In the Power of His Might

Introduction to
**EFFECTIVE
SPIRITUAL WARFARE**

Charles Pretlow

In the Power of His Might
Introduction to Effective Spiritual Warfare

May 2015
Copyright © Charles Pretlow

All rights reserved. Printed in the United States of America. No part of this publication may be reproduced, stored in a retrieval system, or transmitted, in any form or by any means electronic, mechanical, photocopying, recording, or otherwise, without the prior written permission of the author.

Unless otherwise indicated, all Scripture quotations are from the Holy Bible, English Standard Version ® (ESV®), copyright © 2001 by Crossway, a publishing ministry of Good Publishers. Used by permission. All rights reserved.

ISBN 978-1-943412-01-3

Published by -
Wilderness Voice Publishing, LLC
Canon City, Colorado USA
www.wvpbooks.com

About WVP Tract-Book Series

Wilderness Voice Publishing brings this series of short messages on sound doctrine and Christ's teachings to help the sincere Christian shed the many last day false teachings and become mature in the true Christ.

These books are designed to meet the needs of individual disciples, workers, and ministries helping each to become ready for a true and final move of God before Christ appears.

Each book focuses on a specific issue that troubles and confuses many believers today and causes harm to their relationship with Christ. Each author has worked out these very issues qualifying them to bring forth a sound teaching, rightly handling the word of truth. Wilderness Voice Publishing only publishes authors who refuse to tamper with Scripture. Many popular teachers and so called Bible scholars take passages out of context and twist their true meaning. The following passage from the Apostle Paul's letter to the church of Corinth is our mission's banner and our charge:

"We have renounced disgraceful, underhanded ways. We refuse to practice cunning or to tamper with God's word, but by the open statement of the truth we would commend ourselves to everyone's conscience in the sight of God" (2 Corinthians 4:2)

We encourage the reader to carefully study all scripture references and seek the Lord for a clear understanding with a willingness to embrace His discipline.

To that end, may we all *"Attain to the unity of the faith and of the knowledge of God, to mature manhood, to the measure of the stature of the fullness of Christ; so that we may no longer be children, tossed to and fro and carried about by every wind of doctrine, by the cunning of men, by their craftiness in deceitful wiles"* (Ephesians 4:13, 14).

Contents

Chapter 1	Understanding the Enemy's Power	7
Chapter 2	The Full Armor of God	29
Chapter 3	Principalities and Demons	41
Chapter 4	Evil, the Human Spirit and Co-Habitation	71
Chapter 5	Finger of God Power and Prayer	89

About the Author	97
Ministry Information	99
More Books	101

Chapter 1

Understanding the Enemy's Power
A Colossal Shift in our Thinking!

When David stood up to Goliath, he tried to walk towards Israel's nemesis wearing king Saul's armor. David was not familiar with the use of Saul's heavy armament, so David discarded Saul's armor and went with what he was trained in—his staff, a sling, and five smooth stones.

David was trained in fighting lions and bears while tending to his father's sheep alone in the wilderness and that was no he-man feat, but rather, as David put it, *"The LORD who delivered me from the paw of the lion and from the paw of the bear will deliver me from the hand of this Philistine"* (1 Samuel 17:37).

David was no amateur in doing battle against overwhelming odds, against vicious predators more than twice his size. The Lord had trained David for years in preparation for the colossal battle against Goliath and to strike terror into the Philistine army. The Lord trained David, to work in his might in defeating the lion and bear; it was also God's plan to use David later to show Saul and the army of Israel how to defeat the Philistines.

The Lord trained David in solitude; no one saw or helped David learn to trust in the Lord's strength while tending sheep, thus he knew the Lord intimately. This confidence in the Lord would not allow him to be swayed by the unbelief of king Saul. Now David was ready to battle while both armies looked on and stay confident in the Lord only. David single handedly killed the Philistine's championed giant, in the power of God's might and demonstrate to true faith in God to the army of Israel and the king of Israel.

This Old Testament account of doing battle God's way is one of many that the sincere disciple of Christ should be familiar with. Christians must learn how to be trained by the Lord to do spiritual warfare and how to stand up to the giants of darkness. To stand and fight against the hordes of evil people empowered by powerful principalities who oppose God's will and who constantly attack God's people.

True faith in the power of God, formed through experience, obedience and trust was the main part of David's weaponry. Most Christians are thrust into spiritual warfare with man's teachings, magic incantations, a few memorized passages, and a dependence on their own carnal spiritual powers.

Jesus warned that many would exercise spiritual authority over demons using Christ's name, yet not be known by Christ and in the end be rejected as workers of lawlessness. (See Matthew 7:22-23.)

The days are approaching where misguided Christians fighting the powers of darkness in their own carnal spiritual energy, who embrace false doctrines will become fodder for the devil. The time is very near when Satan will change his *playing possum* strategy and turn into a roaring lion destroying many.

A Colossal Shift
The Time has come to Understand True Spiritual Warfare

For decades the emphasis on spiritual warfare has been fighting the powers of darkness to take back America from

1 - Understanding the Enemy's Power

secularism, witches and warlocks, socialism, abortion on demand, and the LGBT culture, and trying to restore prayer in public schools, Christ in Christmas, and family wholesomeness at the Magic Kingdom (Disneyland).

Leadership fell asleep at the wheel and drove God's people into the ditch as angel of light false leaders hijacked the Gospel of Christ. The church of Jesus Christ's love for this world and idolatry of America has grown and now overrides the love for God that gives the ability to abide in his kingdom. This sorrowful condition squelches the effectiveness of God's people to spiritually defeat the powers of darkness and achieve God's will on earth.

Now God's people are at a colossal disadvantage that will require a rude awakening and a major shift in spiritual warfare thinking—if not total disaster awaits.

It is time to understand true spiritual warfare and allow ourselves to become trained and equipped, just as God trained and equipped David during all those years he tended his father's sheep.

David developed a deep faith leading to total reliance on God in conjunction with simple obedience and trust.

Lacking Respect for the Enemy's Power

Until we understand and respect the power of Satan, his fallen angels, the demons, and the devil's people, we will never comprehend the magnitude of God's power or realize the need to walk in that power.

Many times have I heard and read Christian leaders warn not to acknowledge, teach, or even discuss the cunning strategy, powers, or works of the enemy. They minimize the works of hell, fearing that they would give the devil more credit than his due. Even though Jesus and the Apostles made it clear that we are to understand how terrible, far reaching, and deceitful Satan and his minions are—especially in these last days. Most Christians pretend that Biblical reality away.

And that pretending is one of the devil's stratagems to help hide his powers and plans. Christ warned, *"For false christs and false prophets will arise and perform great signs and wonders, so as to lead astray, if possible, even the elect. See, I have told you beforehand"* (Mathew 24:24-25).

Christians are taught to take on spiritual warfare, not having a clue as to what they are really facing. True spiritual warfare will be the most difficult thing we will ever attempt, requiring a process of learning and training; to be led by the Holy Spirit in keen discernment, enduring a regiment of suffering while in training, and dying to one's own self-reliance.

Yes, a new Christian has authority to stand against Satan, as Christ said, "*All authority in heaven and on earth has been given to me*" (Matthew 28:18). God allocates a time of feeding on the milk of the word and protecting young and immature believers from the devil's extreme onslaughts. However, the Lord expects each new believer to gain maturity. Unfortunately, most continue to live on the milk of God's word, *"For everyone who lives on milk is unskilled in the word of righteousness, since he is a child. But solid food is for the mature, for those who have their powers of discernment trained by constant practice to distinguish good from evil"* (Hebrews 5:13-14).

Believers receive delegated authority over Satan and the demonic, provided they are equipped and that they abide in Christ. We are to obey Christ, walk in purity, and follow the Holy Spirit's guidance in all matters, especially in spiritual warfare. There is a fundamental error with

1 - Understanding the Enemy's Power

most teachings concerning spiritual warfare and fighting Satan. Read the following passage carefully.

"Humble yourselves therefore under the mighty hand of God, that in due time he may exalt you. Cast all your anxieties on him for he cares about you. Be sober, be watchful. Your adversary the devil prowls around like a roaring lion, seeking someone to devour. Resist him, firm in your faith, knowing that the <u>same experience of suffering is required of your brotherhood throughout the world</u>. And after you have suffered a little while, the God of all grace, who has called you to his eternal glory in Christ, will himself restore, establish and strengthen you. To him be the dominion forever and ever. Amen" (1 Peter 5:6-11 RSV).

Christian Prosperity and Passivity

Living the carefree and easy life has lulled millions upon millions of Christians asleep, especially in America and other western countries. Few foresee the coming troubles and the grave spiritual weakness that permeates most fellowships.

The blessings we have all grown accustomed to have lulled us into a state of "snoozing" and Satan has taken advantage of this. False prosperity and false eternal security teachings, along with the pre-tribulation rapture theory are the main doctrines inspired by the devil to capture the hearts and minds of the immature believer.

There is now a passive and apathetic approach to discipleship and the discipline of the Lord, resulting in the lack of sincerity in prayer. Millions of believers are bogged down by the cares of this life—in love with the world.

Satan is careful not to disturb this sleep mode until he is ready with his minions to throw God's people into his last days battle plan.

Part of spiritual warfare is learning to discern false doctrine and lying teachers driven by demons. Just as the Apostle Paul describes, *"Now the Spirit expressly says that in later times some will depart from the faith by devoting themselves to deceitful spirits and teachings of demons, through the insincerity of liars whose consciences are seared"* (1 Timothy 4:1-2).

Suffering at the Hands of Satan

In the beginning of our training God allowed us to suffer at the hands of Satan to correct our many misguided perceptions of spiritual warfare and to work into us a permanent humility. If we do not respect Satan's power we will not fear God or desire to abide in Christ, walking in His holiness and in His power.

The fear of God is desperately lacking throughout the body of Christ. Christians do not understand that Satan has permission to buffet, attack, oppress, and challenge Christians for the sake of discipline. Many times Christians take on a satanic issue or a demonic stronghold without regard to God's timing or even knowing God's will in the matter. The results are far-reaching and can be very serious, even resulting in premature loss of life.

Do not be misled into thinking that spiritual warfare is easy and that any Christian will be able to put Satan and demons to flight just by uttering "in the name of Jesus." Remember what happened to the sons of Sceva who invoked the name of our Lord, but who did not personally know Jesus. (See Acts 19:11-17).

On the other hand, Satan often plays possum to allow naïve or arrogant Christians to believe they have great spiritual power and authority over the devil, when actually they have very little—if any.

1 - Understanding the Enemy's Power

Here are a few principles to consider:

- Be humble. Satan devours Christians who think they know it all and walk in spiritual pride and arrogance. Remember what happened to Job and Peter.
- God will raise you up in true authority and power over the works of the devil when you are ready. You must deal with any hidden issues of heart and walk in obedience. You need to have proper understanding with wisdom. Most of all learn to be patient!
- Satan will be allowed to sift you, test you, and attack all that is dear to you. Peter refused to believe he had issues that Satan could use against him. Jesus did not stop Satan from sifting Peter. Idols of the heart will be challenged: relationships, money, education, reputation etc. God will allow these areas of our life to be challenged until all idols of the heart are hammered out of us. The fear of men and the fear of death will be exposed as well.
- When you set out to be obedient, Satan will challenge you every step of the way. Hidden areas of self-confidence are big on Satan's list. Pressing and anxious circumstances will be directed your way that will force you to cast all your cares on God and mean it!
- God requires that all true Christians endure a season of suffering where Satan will be allowed to challenge and sometimes attack. These painful experiences are allowed by the Lord to discipline, train, and strengthen your faith. A deeper purpose is to facilitate cleansing of any hidden defilements and bring to death sin or carnal centered inner personalities. This is training in true spiritual warfare; be attentive, sober-minded, and watchful. Satan will attack and counterattack when and

where you least expect it, *especially when you have had a recent victory*.

• Be encouraged that you are experiencing these challenging trials and battles. The discipline you are receiving is confirmation of acceptance as a son or daughter by your heavenly Father. You are being trained as a true worker and warrior that Satan and demons will respect and fear *in Christ*.

• In this process, Christ's character will be established within you. As you grow in grace and in His righteousness, His power will flow with minimal hindrance (coming from you) and God (in His peace) will crush Satan under you. (See Romans 16:17-20).

• There will be a time when your fight is directed at evil people being used by Satan. Many will be false Christians, and some may even be extended family members. You will learn that spiritual warfare may include prophetic declarations of destruction and premature death for God's people who commit a mortal sin or for an evil person who no longer has faith (those who have a seared conscience and have crossed the line concerning God's saving grace). (See Acts 5:1-11, Acts 8:14-24, Acts 13:4-12, 1 Corinthians 5:1-13, 2 Corinthians 11:12-15, Ephesians 5:1-20, 2 Thessalonians 3:1-5, 1 Timothy 1:18-20, 5:17-22, Titus 1:10-16, 1 John 5:16,17 and Revelation 2:21-29).

Paul ran into powerful resistance in his missions to Asia. Satan was behind these attacks and was used as a tool to bring Paul to the following understanding and discipline.

"For we do not want you to be ignorant, brethren, of the affliction we experienced in Asia; for we were so utterly, unbearably crushed that we despaired of life itself. Why, we felt that we had

1 - Understanding the Enemy's Power

received the sentence of death; but that was to make us rely not on ourselves but on God who raises the dead; he delivered us from so deadly a peril, and he will deliver us; on him we have set our hope that he will deliver us again. You also must help us by prayer, so that many will give thanks on our behalf for the blessing granted us in answer to many prayers" (2 Corinthians 1:8-11).

So expect weaknesses, insults, hardships, persecutions and calamities. In all these things, you will be more than a conqueror and God will deliver you each step of the way. This He will do as long as you are humble, sober-minded, alert, and depending on Him. You must maintain a willingness to continue with a cleansing of all defilements, healing of double-mindedness, and the softening of any hardness of heart.

The body of Christ must have a healthy fear of God restored, which will put an end to so much boastful arrogance and presumption upon God. Be forewarned. There is coming a time in the very near future when Satan will be allowed to severely sift arrogant Christians—in massive numbers.

Persecution is coming on a massive scale and Satan will demand to sift God's people who are in denial of their carnality, double mindedness, and self-powered spiritualism.

Understanding the Enemy

Satan is devious and smart. He loves to puff up Christians, convincing them they are standing when in fact they are one blow away from destruction. Many ministries avoid teaching the schemes and deceit of Satan. Their thought is that this would glorify Satan, so just concentrate on worshiping Christ and adhering to pet doctrines and formulas that maintain prosperity. This approach allows naiveté to prosper where false brethren sneak into fellowship and become Satan's implants causing trouble.

In 2 Peter 2 and from the following passage in Jude, we find some powerful and graphic characteristics of the kind of people Satan enjoys implanting into fellowship.

"These are hidden reefs at your love feasts, as they feast with you without fear, shepherds feeding themselves; waterless clouds, swept along by winds; fruitless trees in late autumn, twice dead, uprooted; wild waves of the sea, casting up the foam of their own shame; wandering stars, for whom the gloom of utter darkness has been reserved forever. We are to take note of people and so-called Christians who create trouble. They do not serve Christ, but their own hidden agendas, and manipulate and deceive naïve Christians with flattery...These are grumblers, malcontents, following their own sinful desires; they are loud-mouthed boasters, showing favoritism to gain advantage. But you must remember, beloved, the predictions of the apostles of our Lord Jesus Christ. They said to you, 'In the last time there will be scoffers, following their own ungodly passions." It is these who cause divisions, worldly people, devoid of the Spirit" (Jude 1:12-29).

Further, the Apostle Paul repeatedly warned us in his writings to identify, take note, and avoid such people.

Often Christians unknowingly give opportunity to Satan by harboring resentment, unforgiveness, or hanging onto unresolved anger. Maintaining sinful alliances or having secret sins, gives Satan place to come and tempt and even destroy. In addition, if you have impure motives in life or disregard sound doctrine pertaining to healthy fellowship and matters of proper relationships, you can expect trouble.

1 - Understanding the Enemy's Power

Satan loves to use unclean and defiling people who worm their way into relationships and become entangled with naïve and carnal Christians.

Understanding the Full Extent of Evil

The word *evil* is now used commonly in the secular arena, in politics, and is used to describe the increase in worldwide human atrocities. However, for the church of Jesus Christ, the word *evil* is seldom used in describing the ills and scandals surfacing throughout Christianity. Few believers are taught or study the descriptive warnings found in Christ's words or the Apostles writings in the New Testament.

Few Christians comprehend the extent of evil in society and the many evils that are hidden right in their own fellowship. The following passage from Romans explains the importance of discerning evil cloaked in decency that eventually causes problems, especially for the naïve, yet sincere Christian.

"I appeal to you, brothers, to watch out for those who cause divisions and create obstacles contrary to the doctrine that you have been taught; <u>avoid them</u>. For such persons do not serve our Lord Christ, but their own appetites, and by smooth talk and flattery they deceive the hearts of the naive. For your obedience is known to all, so that I rejoice over you, but I want you to be wise as to what is good and innocent [no longer deceived] as to what is evil. The God of peace will soon crush Satan under your feet. The grace of our Lord Jesus Christ be with you" (Romans 16:17-20 [emphasis added for clarity]).

The Apostle Paul plainly warns about evil people implanted by the devil in this passage. Further, how these people pretend to serve Christ, but really have a hidden agenda. Paul explains that this type of person uses flattery to deceive naïve believers due to their ignorance on detecting evil disguised as good. Importantly, Paul encourages us that when Satan's work is exposed (as we become wise as to what is truly good, no longer deceived as to what is evil,) then Satan's work will be crushed by God. Unfortunately, few desire to work with the Lord on that level of commitment in order to gain maturity and victory.

Jesus trained his disciples by allowing an evil person to work beside them right up to the end. He referred to Judas as a devil, knowing from the beginning what the betrayer would do. Christ allowed the disciples to experience firsthand how evil can be hidden with a cloak of decency.

Deceived by the Anointing

The Apostles were taught and trained by Christ and Judas Iscariot was one of their toughest lessons. Judas walked in the power of God to cast out demons and heal the sick, yet he was a devil from the beginning.

Concerning false believers like Judas, Jesus warned, *"On that day many will say to me, 'Lord, Lord, did we not prophesy in your name, and cast out demons in your name, and do many mighty works in your name?' And then will I declare to them, 'I never knew you; depart from me, you workers of lawlessness.'"* (Matthew 7:22-13).

We see in Scripture how the end of this age will bring powerful deceptions with false signs and wonders *within Christianity*. In this passage Jesus did not disagree with these workers of lawlessness as to having spiritual power to cast out demons, prophesy, or that they used Christ's name in all their charismatic exploits.

1 - Understanding the Enemy's Power

So Jesus used Judas to train his disciples in discerning so-called Christians who played games—who in reality were false and evil.

Consequently, when evil tried to invade the church just after the day of Pentecost, Peter did not hesitate to allow the Holy Spirit to use him to convey a death sentence to fall upon Ananias and Sapphira. These two were game players who, out of jealousy and greed for recognition, lied about their donation to the early church. Peter understood the seriousness of this when he heard from the Holy Spirit concerning their agreed upon lie. This was an aspect of the early Church spiritual warfare many ignore today.

Unfortunately, evil disguised as good and often appearing to be anointed with power has invaded the Church of Jesus Christ because most leaders avoid Christ's training in discernment and executing God's will in the power of the Holy Spirit.

And everywhere in society, evil is ever growing with demon possession, demon cohabitation, and the so-called mentally ill spewing forth nightmarish horrors in the daily news—frequent mass murders, crime, and diabolical wickedness are becoming normal daily occurrences.

Indeed, the Apostle Paul warned, *"But understand this, that in the last days there will come times of difficulty. For people will be lovers of self, lovers of money, proud, arrogant, abusive, disobedient to their parents, ungrateful, unholy, heartless, unappeasable, slanderous, without self-control, brutal, not loving good, treacherous, reckless, swollen with conceit, lovers of pleasure rather than lovers of God, having the appearance of godliness, but denying its power. Avoid such people"* (2 Timothy 3:1-5).

Exposing Hidden Darkness

When we are willing and ready to do battle for God, we can expect the Lord to lead us into exposing hidden evils around us.

CAUTION: This activity can be a shock. There were cases when we exposed evil, where relatives, close friends and other Christians became directly affected; and occasionally they themselves were the instruments of evil.

Evil is real and evil people exist. Evil likes to hide and burrow deep into family systems, perpetuated by generational sins. God wants these things exposed.

"Therefore be imitators of God, as beloved children. And walk in love, as Christ loved us and gave himself up for us, a fragrant offering and sacrifice to God. But fornication and all impurity or covetousness must not even be named among you, as is fitting among saints. Let there be no filthiness, nor silly talk, nor levity, which are not fitting; but instead let there be thanksgiving. Be sure of this, that no fornicator or impure man, or one who is covetous (that is, an idolater), has any inheritance in the kingdom of Christ and of God. Let no one deceive you with empty words, for it is because of these things that the wrath of God comes upon the sons of disobedience. Therefore do not associate with them, for once you were darkness, but now you are light in the Lord; walk as children of light (for the fruit of light is found in all that is good and right and true), and try to learn what is pleasing to the Lord. <u>Take no part in the unfruitful works of darkness, but instead expose them</u>. For it is a shame even to speak of the things that they do in secret; but when anything is exposed by the light it becomes visible, for anything that becomes visible is light. Therefore it is said, 'Awake, O sleeper, and arise from the dead, and Christ shall give you light.' Look carefully then how you walk, not as unwise men but as

1 - Understanding the Enemy's Power

wise, making the most of the time, because the days are evil. Therefore do not be foolish, but understand what the will of the Lord is" (Ephesians 5:1-17).

Yes, the days are evil, and evil people do evil things in secret! Be careful and be diligent in learning discernment from the Lord. Remember, Jesus warned about judging wrongly. The following principle will help you understand and seek proper discernment of evil.

> Many sinners do evil, but have faith and a good heart that will respond to the Gospel when prayer is offered on their behalf. At times, an intercessor must stand in the gap for them. These will respond to effective witnessing, truly renounce their evil practices and grow in the grace of the Lord. The Holy Spirit must lead, which will require keen discernment when working with such people because ...
>
> Evil people look like any sinner, but do evil from the heart and have a seared conscience. Many in this condition will never be granted repentance by the Lord. They may respond to testimony, come to church and attempt to be religious, only to be false through and through. Some look very righteous and even do good deeds. Their self-righteous evil builds up themselves at the expense of others and in the process destroys life and faith in others. This is true evil; it is to be exposed, confronted, avoided, and if there is no fruit of repentance, then they must be driven out of fellowship!

Many pastors cry out for revival and then the cleansing pre-revival activity of God begins to occur, most often trouble comes upon the congregation. Adultery is exposed, fights break out, schisms develop, roots of bitterness spring up, and a host of other sin and carnal problems crop up. One major issue is domestic violence, which is born from marriage troubles that finally comes to the surface. Sadly, in some cases family pedophilia is exposed.

This actually indicates that prayer for revival is working. The wicked, corrupt, and wayward, which are in needful of correction, are coming to the light as the Holy Spirit begins cleaning house in preparation for revival and adding souls to the fellowship.

Many congregations are perfect hideouts for child molesters. Abuse toward children—physically, emotionally and sexually—is at an epidemic level within Christian homes just as it is in our society as a whole.

Far too many Christians and pastors tend to let sleeping dogs lie and avoid exposing any evil that is lurking within the flock. They do not want scandal, trouble, gossip, and irate howling relatives when the church holds an abusive husband or wife, father or mother, grandfather or grandmother accountable. Most churches are under the influence of the uncrucified sin nature and learn to prefer hypocrisy and leave evil hidden. They want to present themselves to the community as a wonderful rosy-pictured congregation walking in unity, *a Shangri-la portrait full of pretense!*

Sound preaching and teaching of the entire Gospel and embracing the work of the cross will create a supportive atmosphere within the congregation. This facilitates true Christian healing and restoration. The congregation will

1 - Understanding the Enemy's Power

rise above the worry of what others think, and as Christ did by *despising the shame*, when working in messy situations and receiving flack for doing the perfect will of God as darkness and evil are exposed.

In some cases, the exposed evil can bring repercussions to the whole community, as well as the local church. Nevertheless, the command is *expose darkness* and drive that which is wicked from fellowship is still in force by the Lord. Exposing hidden evil in our community and society, including all institutions, is also the responsibility of the praying and warring saint.

Magic Formulas Won't Work Any More

We are clearly in the last days where Sodom type perversions are spewing out everywhere. Demonic activity is increasing and enlisting the personal spirits of evil and unclean humans, including carnal and false Christians.

Lot and his family were vexed to the very core of their beings. This kind of vexation and demonic activity is upon us now and will increase more than that of the days of Lot. As the end-of-this-age unfolds, Satan is in the process of being thrown out of heaven and he is coming down in great wrath.

Is there a vexation within you from what you are experiencing? Then there are defilements from your past still lodged within your soul and spirit. If you play church and practice a mental pretend game with yourself concerning the full armor of God or pleading the blood of Christ or any other superstitious quick-fix gimmick, you are in for the shock of your life.

If you believe you can just "praise" these coming attacks off, you are mistaken. Merely because you tithe faithfully, attend church regularly, or are in the ministry—these activities will not exempt you from the oncoming satanic onslaught.

No, you must go through the discipline of the Lord. You must experience firsthand God's penetrating work in your heart and spirit where He tests and sometimes sends fiery trials that will purge, cleanse and heal the deep wounds and defilements in which so many Christians suffer. You must allow Christ to expose any and all defilements hidden within. (See 2 Corinthians 7:1.)

Do not condemn yourself when the Lord exposes the hidden and do not be shocked, but take ownership and confess its ugliness. Partner with likeminded Christians and hold each other accountable to press in, confess issues, pray with one another and trust in God's faithfulness.

This is humbling, but God will grant cleansing, healing and restoration. Humble yourself before God and He will exalt you.

How Satan Plays Possum

One of Satan's favorite tricks is to deceive. Like the Trojan horse, the enemy of our soul has come into our camp as an angel of light and a worker of righteousness. (See 2 Corinthians 11:12-15.)

Satan sends in false apostles, carnal ministers, and wayward teachers who are deceitful and disguised as believers of Christ. The apostle Paul referred to false apostles as superlative apostles who boast as though they worked on the same level as a true apostle.

These same type of imposters are everywhere in the body of Christ today, and they amaze millions of

1 - Understanding the Enemy's Power

Christians. Miracles abound, tricking many to believe these false teachers and their false teachings.

Millions of Christians are fooled by these false apostles and prophets and follow after them because so few truly love God with all their heart and earnestly seek to follow Christ and know his voice.

"If a prophet or a dreamer of dreams arises among you and gives you a sign or a wonder, and the sign or wonder that he tells you comes to pass, and if he says, 'Let us go after other gods,' which you have not known, 'and let us serve them,' you shall not listen to the words of that prophet or that dreamer of dreams. For the LORD your God is testing you, to know whether you love the LORD your God with all your heart and with all your soul. You shall walk after the LORD your God and fear him and keep his commandments and obey his voice, and you shall serve him and hold fast to him" (Deuteronomy 13:1-4).

Signs and wonders follow these so-called great men and women of God, but in reality the spiritual power brought forth is straight from hell. In many cases, Satan gladly exchanges an outer physical ailment for a hell-inspired doctrine. The physical ailments and problems seem healed, at least temporarily, but the soul and spirit are now in grave danger of severe deception empowered by a supernatural religious demon and/or a demonic principality.

Leaders of these *angel of light* ministries have a counterfeit faith, about which the apostle Paul warned Timothy to watch out for. (See 2 Timothy 3:1-9). Satan plays dead, like a possum, so that later he can really destroy the deceived. He will begin calling on all those who have embraced false doctrines and entertained demonic counterfeiting powers as the work of the Holy

Spirit. Already, we have witnessed one shameful scandal after another from pulpits and national leadership positions all across the country.

Those who went along with these *angel of light* ministries will fall into trouble and temptation so intense that the attacks will destroy what faith is left or hopefully awaken the deceived believer to the truth. The deceived and gullible will encounter more trouble, as Satan will attempt to drag them down, but God is faithful and will save those who wake up and repent in time.

Part of the discipline that comes at the hand of God is learning to stand against evil and resist the devil. Through trials and battles with the demonic, we grow up into a true faith in Christ, having His nature become ours, learning to hear his voice and obey.

Praying magic incantations is not a substitute for the discipline of the Lord that produces a full relationship with Christ. Christ's shed blood is not some magic potion delivered by God for Christians to spray at the devil like a fire hose.

Case in point: I recently counseled a very wounded and troubled Christian. She just could not get a grasp on what was going on and how so many problems continued to come her way. At one point in our conversations she told me that she "pleaded buckets of blood" over her troubling situation to no avail.

The blood of Christ was given for the forgiveness of sins, not to be applied mysteriously over stressful situations, demonic attacks, and material property. This superstitious act is like the Roman Catholic doctrine of the Eucharist where the priest, through ceremony and special prayer, invokes the transubstantiation of the blood and

1 - Understanding the Enemy's Power

body of Christ into wine and wafers. This is a foul doctrine inspired by demons, as is the false doctrine of pleading of the blood of Christ.

The prayer that magically puts on the full armor of God is another superstitious myth and incantation that does nothing.

Oh, Satan loves to play possum and pretend these myths and incantations work. Later he will come and destroy; uprooting these deceived Christians like tumbleweeds in a storm.

We are to *put* on the armor of God, not *pray* it on magically. Putting on the armor of God is done through the discipline of the Lord.

For example, the breastplate of righteousness is part of the armor of God mentioned in Scripture and it means putting on true righteousness from the heart. This requires unbelief, impurity, and other defilements within the heart to come to the light (our awareness) to be dealt with. Working with the Lord and applying the whole armor of God is covered later in the following chapter.

Anointing everything with oil for protection is another error. In the Old Testament certain people were anointed with oil symbolizing being set apart for God's purposes. New Testament accounts direct the use of oil to be used to anoint the sick for healing. There is the anointing of the Holy Spirit upon all true believers for understanding, wisdom, and the love of God. Many people think that walking in the gifts of the Holy Spirit makes them special, as someone anointed of God. Remember, God is no respecter of persons. Don't fall for this false doctrine either.

Chapter 2

The Full Amor of God
Ephesians 6:10-20

When properly worked into us the full armor of God allows a true disciple to fight victoriously. Demons will know and fear that Christian who is truly in Christ and whom Christ works through, not what that Christian says or commands in his own carnal volition!

The full armor of God that most Christians are led to believe they have put on (I must say, they attempt to magically put on God's armor) will not stop the vexing evil that is now being unleashed.

The "quick-fix" doctrines that avoid inner sanctification and cleansing will be no match for this flood of filth and spiritual oppression. The landslide of filth that Christians are now exposed to will penetrate into the spirit and soul of those who do not wear the true armor of God—those who avoided the fires of sanctification.

As the end of this age unfolds, Scripture clearly describes and warns that the devil and his minions will exercise great power with signs, wonders, and evil powers to deceive, entrap, and destroy.

As Christians we must understand fully how to walk in God's protection and apply His whole armor in order to stand in His power against the spiritual forces of darkness. Many take for granted the power of Christ that is available when we abide in Christ. Far too many abide in Christ partially, and many only know of Christ by name and use His name haphazardly.

Most people know the name of their favorite actor or actress, but they have never met them personally. And that is the case with many believers in Christ. They have heard of him and know a great amount of information about him and certainly know of Christ's name and how to use his name in prayer, but they have never met him personally.

Not personally knowing Christ is a serious condition for many Christians, as Jesus warned of those believers who were locked out of eternity. Jesus said to them, "*I never knew you.*" (See Matthew 7:21-23 and Matthew 25:1-13).

Magically chanting to put on the full armor of God is absolutely ludicrous and invites eventual disaster. We must understand that we are to know Christ intimately and be known by him and become transformed by him to be like him—then the armor of God becomes reality.

The Apostle Paul's use of military personnel armament points to each piece covering vital parts of the body. The analogy is having Christ-like attributes of truth, righteousness, peace, faith, salvation, abiding in the Holy Spirit, the word of God, and alertly praying at all times in the Spirit equated to full body armor worn by soldiers.

These Christ-like attributes are our armor and cannot be put on by pretending and are vital to our wellbeing and physical safety in fighting against the powers of darkness. Christians are to work out their own salvation and grow up into Christ. Many try take on Satan's territory in immaturity and in their own spiritual power not having gained these listed Christ-like attributes to be put into their character. This leads to folly and destruction.

Passivity, impurities of heart, a double-minded condition, and carnal energy when doing spiritual warfare is like trying to put out a fire with a can of gasoline. This is

2 - The Full Amor of God

the condition for most Christians and Satan loves the naïve, deceived and arrogant to take him on knowing these believers will do him little to no harm.

What is missing in the Christian's warfare training is how to embrace the work of the cross in the believer's life, which is vital in dying to the hidden carnal motives and self-strength that drives carnal spiritual powers.

In Christ's army, as in any military, one cannot do their own thing. Jesus is to be our master and commander-in-chief, and we are not to be led by flamboyant superlative apostles who capture God's people to follow them.

The Apostle Paul warned, *"I know that after my departure fierce wolves will come in among you, not sparing the flock; and from among your own selves will arise men speaking twisted things, to draw away the disciples after them. Therefore be alert, remembering that for three years I did not cease night or day to admonish every one with tears"* (Acts 20:29-31).

Many have little patience or the ability to endure suffering in warfare and of those there are many who retreat in the face of the enemy and leave their post. Leaving one's post when on guard duty or combat is a serious offence.

The Apostle Paul's analogy of military armor and discipline must be understood in order to put on and be worn correctly. This is done by Christ training and discipline, where Christ-like character is the core of each warring saint's life.

Praying in the Holy Spirit at all Times
Not In Our Own Spirit-Power Driven by Carnal Motives

One of the most deceitful and insidious works upon the church of Jesus Christ by the devil has been the infusion of false teachings that misdirect Christians from praying in the Holy Spirit. Over the last forty plus years new age, eastern mysticism, and pagan spiritual practices has subtly ensnared most Pentecostal and Charismatic believers into learning to pray in their own spirit.

One of the current fads is called soul soaking, where a certain genre of worship music is listened to help relax. The following describes this new age middle east method creeping into Christian teachings:

> 'Soaking worship' or 'soaking prayer' as it is sometimes called, is focused time communing with God, facilitated by the new genre of Christian music generally referred to as 'soaking music'; music written, played and sung by the new psalmists, characterized by relaxing, peaceful, gentle tones and harmonies.
>
> We know from experience that a wonderful way to relax is soaking in a warm bath while listening to quiet, soothing music in an atmosphere of soft candles and beautiful aromas. It creates a peaceful, serene interlude.
>
> Physical immersion in the water and the calming atmosphere separate us from the demands of the day, enabling us to let go of tension and stress. It is a soothing, quiet time apart where we can relax, become centered, regain our inner harmony and emerge refreshed.
>
> Soul soaking and soaking worship takes simple meditation to a higher spiritual experience. It is a time apart with the Lord to become immersed in His presence, to soak in His love, to feel His living water flowing through us and all around us, returning us to peace and well-being.
>
> Soaking worship music has the power to move us emotionally and spiritually in ways that usher us into the presence of the Lord. The music helps us quiet our minds and relax our bodies, taking us out of our heads where we are consumed with everyday challenges, and back

2 - The Full Amor of God

into our hearts where we can more easily receive and feel God's love and the joy of life.

This new age practice disguised as worship and meditation is carnal spiritualism leading to a counterfeit demonic entrance.

Soul soaking, slain in the Spirit, wild and exotic manifestations, and other such carnal spiritual practices start out as mild fringe movements and quickly grow into a consuming lust for the *anointing power* exhibited by even more strange pagan-like activity.

The root of these false teachings that are producing strange manifestations (such as involuntary jerking, maddening antics, uncontrollable laughing, ecstatic feelings, and rolling and squirming on the floor) come from a deep misunderstanding of what it means to pray in the Holy Spirit.

We are to pray at all times in the Holy Spirit, *"Praying at all times in the Spirit, with all prayer and supplication. To that end keep alert with all perseverance, making supplication for all the saints"* (Ephesians 6:18).

Unfortunately, greedy for the power of God for all the wrong reasons (like Simon the Magician in Acts 8:9-24), most Charismatic and Pentecostal believers have been misled to engage their own personal spirit as a substitute for the true manifestation of the Holy Spirit.

Through false teachings and counterfeiting demonic forces, deceived Christians are led to succumb to a spiritual awakening within their own spirit—apart from the Holy Spirit.

The manifestations described previously (uncontrolled jerking, shaking, and feelings of ecstasy) are uncannily the same as those encountered in Hinduism and referred to as a Kundalini awakening.

The work of the cross in the form of dying to our carnal passions and desires of our flesh, as well as embracing all the teachings of Christ in his discipline for all of life, will bring us discernment. We will learn to discern our own spirit manifesting its own peculiar or strange physical and emotional sensations that are erratic and uncontrolled, against the fruit of the Holy Spirit as listed in Scripture.

In the discipline of the Lord we learn to resist taking shortcuts in seeking and walking in the fruit of the Spirit and eventually expunge any and all carnal spiritualism that Satan and false doctrines may have led us toward.

"But the fruit of the Spirit is love, joy, peace, patience, kindness, goodness, faithfulness, gentleness, self-control; against such things there is no law. And those who belong to Christ Jesus have crucified the flesh with its passions and desires" (Galatians 5:22-24).

Seeking shortcuts, to the fruit of the Holy Spirit's presence and the power gifts of the Holy Spirit, has created a gigantic opening for counterfeiting spirits of the demonic to invade millions upon millions of deceived Christians.

Ministries have risen to prominence operating in counterfeit anointing, imparting false manifestations along with signs and wonders—all orchestrated by the devil.

Defensive Warfare

The concept of defensive warfare is simple. Like defensive driving, we must be on the alert at all times.

As Peter wrote, *"<u>Humble yourselves</u> therefore under the mighty hand of God, that in due time he may exalt you. Cast all your <u>anxieties</u> on him, for he cares about you. Be <u>sober</u>, be <u>watchful</u>.*

2 - The Full Amor of God

Your adversary the devil prowls around like a roaring lion, seeking someone to devour. Resist him, firm <u>in your faith, knowing</u> that the same experience of <u>suffering is required</u> of your brotherhood throughout the world. And after you have suffered a little while, the God of all grace, who has called you to his eternal glory in Christ, will himself <u>restore, establish, and strengthen</u> you. To him be the dominion forever and ever. Amen" (1 Peter 5:6-11).

The emphasized areas in the above text are my highlights and are the basic attitudes and actions required for day-to-day living as a Christian. I also emphasized the divine benefits. Faithful adherence is required. If you submit to the training and discipline of the Lord and consistently practice defensive warfare principles, you will be ready when evil comes near.

There are times when God will grant us *rest and recreation* and we can temporarily lower our defenses and relax. Unfortunately, we are a generation that loves leisure, entertainment, and rest—returning to a proper warfare stance after a time-out is often difficult. We become passive in our warfare, and we then wonder why we are surprised at the success of the enemy's attack.

Again, defensive warfare requires constant humility, soberness in all things, and keeping constant vigilance. When Satan attacks you, resist him in faith, the faith that relies on God and not on self or on religious prayers. God is not pleased with the hardhearted Christians who give him lip service. These people do spiritual warfare by rote.

They babble faithless incantations, such as pleading the blood over themselves or magically don the armor of God to fend off the demonic. This type of Christian refuses to admit that they may have carnal character structures and foul motives in serving God, allowing Satan the right to harass and torment.

A reminder: *The practice of saying a prayer that pleads the blood of Christ stems from the belief that Christ's blood, shed on the cross (once and for all), can be mystically directed to cover a person, situation or material element for protection. This is similar to the Roman Catholic practice where the priest speaks a mystical prayer (transubstantiation) whereby the bread and wine of the Eucharist are transformed into the body and blood of Jesus, although its appearances remain the same.*

You must remember that suffering will be involved. Sometimes it will be impossible to endure (humanly speaking), thus we grow to rely on His grace and not our own carnal spiritual strength.

Yes, our success is by God's unmerited grace; however, we must work out our own salvation and become obedient in all things. We learn obedience from the heart through the discipline of the Lord and partaking in the sufferings for Christ. We become motivated to love God unconditionally, not to accumulate points that allow boasting in His presence. (See Hebrews 5:7-10).

Offensive Warfare

There are times when God calls us to attack. We must allow God to crush the enemy's work through our prayers and wrestling (suffering) and occasionally Christ may require that we turn someone over to Satan for discipline. This may end up causing premature death. (Review the Apostle Paul's letters to the Christians at Corinth.)

We may be involved in confronting evil people, as did Peter when he dealt with Ananias and Sapphira. Training and discipline tempers our ability, boldness, and spiritual

2 - The Full Amor of God

skills to wrestle with the powers of darkness and destroy strongholds, expose evil and evil people and sometimes confront sin straight on. As we walk in a defensive posture, we must not shy away from attacking evil and the powers of darkness when instructed to do so by our Heavenly Father.

Those who proactively take on Satan must do so with a clear mandate from God. Foolish pride and presumptuous arrogance is a trap for carnal Christians. Fellowships that attempt to take on Satan's territory apart from the Holy Spirit's leadership and guidance will be subjected to severe trouble that could result in destruction, even loss of life.

If there is secret sin in the camp, the congregation and even leadership can expect to get a real beating. When false brethren join in on the effort, for whatever reason, there will be unnecessary casualties. Never enlist immature Christians to do this kind of warfare. Do not; I say again, *do not* involve Christians who are not likeminded or have not submitted to the discipline of the Lord and the work of the cross.

Christians who take on the enemy knowingly must be seasoned prayer warriors and true disciples who maintain a stable walk with Christ. Even then, one can expect suffering and more discipline.

Remember, Jesus commanded His disciples to wait until power came upon them before they went out to fulfill the Great Commission. They had been prepared for this power, so we also must be prepared in the discipline of the Lord for this same power. We must embrace the work of the cross so that our day of Pentecostal power might come, in the time of His choosing. This includes being commissioned with spiritual power in combating evil and the prince of the air's darkest work.

"He gives power to the faint, and to him who has no might he increases strength. Even youths shall faint and be weary, and young men shall fall exhausted; but they who wait for the LORD shall renew their strength, they shall mount up with wings like eagles, they shall run and not be weary, they shall walk and not faint" (Isaiah 40:29-31).

The Sword of the Spirit
Holy Spirit-Led Engagement

Christians who decide to wrestle against evil must understand the difference between applying memorized verses of Scripture in spiritual battle as opposed to the word of God, quickened by the Holy Spirit.

Paul wrote that we are to take up *"...the sword of the Spirit, which is the **word** of God"* (Ephesians 6:17), as we stand against the evil dark forces in heavenly places.

I have highlighted "word" in this passage to point out a difference. In this case, the Greek for "word" is *rhema*, which is different from other usages of "word." This implies a direct command by the Holy Spirit as He quickens to memory the appropriate written word of God to apply in each situation.

"The significance of rhema (as distinct from logos) is exemplified in the injunction to "take the sword of the Spirit which is the word of God," in Eph. 6:17. Here the reference is not to the whole Bible as such, but to the individual Scripture which the Spirit brings to our remembrance for use in time of need, a prerequisite being the regular storing of the mind with Scripture" (*Vine's Expository Dictionary of Biblical Words*, Thomas Nelson Publishers NY 1985. page 683).

2 - The Full Amor of God

When Christians lack sound doctrine to aid in rightly dividing the written word of God, then the memorization of the Scriptures will be out of context. This will hinder the Holy Spirit's efforts to bring to remembrance appropriate Scripture that would reflect God's will on a particular situation.

Many Christians apply Scripture out of context when they do spiritual warfare. They fall out of God's timing and purpose, and in some cases actually oppose the will of God.

Some pray for God's protection for people, when in fact God has turned them over to judgment and in like manner the reverse often occurs as well, where Christians turn people over to judgment in prayer, when they were to stand in the gap for that person.

Christ will discipline us to correctly understand God's word and hear from the Holy Spirit accurately. Discerning the true voice of the Holy Spirit is paramount to the success in *taking up the sword of the Spirit.*

Chapter 3

Principalities and Demons

Identifying Principalities

Over the years many movements have come and gone concerning spiritual warfare and prayer. I remember Larry Lea's program in the late eighties. This movement attempted to network parts of the body of Christ into a massive organized spiritual warfare system on a national level.

God did not back this effort. Satan delights in beating up Christians who take him on in the flesh. (See Acts 19:11-17). This carnal attempt at spiritual warfare was stopped— *right in its tracks*! Its last campaign I remember was that of taking on the witches in the San Francisco area.

The plan was to identify the different principalities that were gripping different communities and then launch an all-out assault, enlisting local congregations and Christians in the community to pray. Rallies were held and large amounts of donations were received to get this national movement off the ground. This effort to identify and fight the forces of darkness and principalities ended in failure, scandal, and destruction—after 27 years of marriage, Larry filed for divorce in April 1999.

The World Prayer Center in Colorado Springs, hosted by New Life Church, promoted spiritual mapping and facilitated a worldwide prayer network—amounting to carnal spiritualism having no effect on Satan's powers.

Review of the many different prayer groups, spiritual war campaigns, and the humanistic atmosphere will send chills through the discerning saint. The New Life Prayer Center like so many others was and is another carnal attempt to enlist an army of carnal prayer warriors to take on Satan's strongholds. The dollars spent and massive number of deceived workers involved in these misguided efforts will not withstand Satan's sifting in the coming days.

Any attempt to take on opposing principalities must be done under the direction of the Lord and by solid disciples who are ready to endure suffering, trouble, persecution, blackmail, harassment, frequent physical misery, and mental anguish.

Paul wrote of his mission into Asia and the opposition that he encountered, *"For we do not want you to be ignorant, brethren, of the affliction we experienced in Asia; for we were so utterly, unbearably crushed that we despaired of life itself. Why, we felt that we had received the sentence of death; but that was to make us rely not on ourselves but on God who raises the dead; he delivered us from so deadly a peril, and he will deliver us; on him we have set our hope that he will deliver us again. You also must help us by prayer, so that many will give thanks on our behalf for the blessing granted us in answer to many prayers"* (2 Corinthians 1:8-11).

Many Scriptures point to a required purity of heart in fighting the demonic, and the warfare must be directed by God. In addition, it is to be carried out by those who have counted the cost. Intercessors and Christian workers are in high demand in this great fight. These people cannot be just anybody. The call of God is the prerequisite, and they must experience the refining fires of sanctification. (See Ephesians 4:25-30, Romans 16 verses 17-20, 2 Corinthians 2:9-11, 2 Corinthians 4:7-10, 1 Thessalonians 2:7-18, Revelation 2:10, and 1 Peter 5:6-11).

3 - Principalities and Demons

Many of the prosperity and hyper-faith leaders contend that the apostle Paul was ignorant of the power of God and that the personal suffering described by this true apostle was unnecessary. How arrogant and deceived are these modern day charlatans! The audacity to declare an author of the Scriptures to be in error because his accounts in Scripture do not fit into their spiritual warfare gimmicks—this is indeed heresy!

We must learn what the Scriptures teach, and we are to understand the cost of doing God's will in spiritual warfare. Some of these errant teachings come up with the wildest descriptions of the demonic and of the spiritual powers controlling people, communities, and nations.

The main names of the principalities are the names of the false gods and idols worshipped by the Gentiles in biblical times. Through the years and in different cultures, their names have changed. To give an example, Asherah worship—found in Canaan—along with Baal worship entered into Israel's temple worship.

Asherah idol worship closely resembles Ishtar and Isis worship found in Babylon and Egypt respectively. Later, this female false god appeared in Greek and Roman mythology. In New Testament times, Asherah was "Diana of the Ephesians" and today it has entered into the Catholic Church as "Mary, mother of God—Queen of Heaven."

Further, you can see this impact in our culture with the resurrection of these principalities in the TV characters such as She-Rah, Isis, Wonder Woman and so forth. The male counterparts traced into our culture are Baal, Hercules, and Superman.

Certain principalities continue to spawn the Middle East crisis. These satanic powers are determined to destroy Israel. In the book of Daniel, it states that the prince of Persia (a demonic governing power over Persia) opposed the archangel Michael and delayed God's answer to Daniel's prayers concerning the release of Israel from their captivity.

Ancient Persia is modern day Iran, and look how that same principality (fallen angel) is working to destroy the whole nation of Israel.

Baal and Asherah worship is the biblical counterpart to relationship idolatry. The name Baal means husband, owner of the wife and Asherah means wife. This kind of idolatry swept into Israel. Soon this idolatry mingled into their worship of God. You can see Satan's work continues on from Adam and Eve, where he told Eve, *"you will be like God"*, into what we term relationship idolatry. These relationship issues stem from making each other a god in varying issues of life. This results in each spouse requiring the other to be responsible for inner peace, joy, and happiness, leading to weaknesses and dependencies.

These carnal and selfish relationship dynamics become destructive, controlling, and manipulative where each learns how to dominate the other. The current legalistic submission teachings, concerning husbands and wives within many denominations, which demand the wife be submissive and treated as a second-class creation, are the work of these principalities.

Moloch was another pagan cult god worshipped in Biblical times. This pagan cult god was a more radical form of Baal and Asherah worship where children were made to walk into fire as a sacrifice. Today child abuse, child abductions, abandonment, child rape and child pornography are widespread.

There is an epidemic of child molestation in different Christian sects. The Roman Catholic heresy of celibacy and other sick doctrines facilitate a *harbor of safety* for the wicked and the pedophile. Of late, offshoots of Mormonism are being exposed for their wayward doctrines that facilitate, and yet conceal the practices of polygamy and sexual child abuse.

Christian workers, intercessors, and those in ministry who graduate from Christ's training course will enable Christ's authority to flow through with minimal carnal hindrance. The sold-out warrior of Christ will break the demonic strongholds in the lives of the people within their community, families, and the congregations.

Remember, though we are warring against satanic principalities who spiritually rule in darkness, we must also understand that people are their pawns, victims, and agents who channel for the forces of darkness.

Archetype Mindsets
Conscious and Unconscious Prejudice, Unbelief, and Misbelief

We must understand thoroughly what the Apostle Paul meant when he wrote, *"See to it that no one takes you captive by philosophy and empty deceit, according to human tradition, according to the elemental spirits of the world, and not according to Christ"* (Colossians 2:8).

And here in this passage, *"For though we walk in the flesh, we are not waging war according to the flesh. For the weapons of our warfare are not of the flesh but have divine power to destroy strongholds. We destroy arguments and every lofty opinion raised against the knowledge of God, and take every thought captive to obey Christ, being ready to punish every disobedience, when your obedience is complete"* (2 Corinthians 10:3-6).

One of the most subtle works of darkness by the fallen angels is their tireless efforts in creating and perpetuating prejudicial thinking, which engulfs whole human cultures Some archetype thinking are male and female attitude and perceptions they have of each other, about religions, toward children, between races and throughout Christianity.

It is these demonically inspired archetype mindsets that capture millions into believing falsities about God, themselves, others, and life's origins and purposes.

Defined, a archetype mindset is the acting out of deep seated wrong thinking amongst groups of people. It takes the form of deceitful philosophy, or a way of thinking that becomes a habitual mindset. These archetype mindsets, when embraced and perpetuated can grip the free will thinking of otherwise intelligent people.

The following are some common examples of archetype mindsets:

- Hitler's philosophy concerning the Aryan race and how he viewed other certain races as being inferior. Racial prejudices are still deep seated throughout many cultures in spite of all the destruction it has caused.
- Thinking that the Jewish people and the state of Israel are the reason for the stress and continuous wars in the Middle East is another archetype mindset.
- Homosexuality as a mistake of gender at conception or at birth is another that is ever growing.

3 - Principalities and Demons

- Evolution and the order of species as scientific proof that humans were not created by God is a powerful anti-God, anti-creation mindset.
- Extraterrestrial beings existing as part of God's plan of creation. This mindset nullifies Scripture that clearly points to ET encounters and historical artifacts of ET, as fallen angel activity taking the form of physical and paranormal manifestations.
- Another predominate and pervasive archetype mindset is the lie that females are created to be less intelligent and less valuable than males.
- Another destructive principality controlled mindset is the lie that the husband or the wife is responsible for their spouse's self-image and sense of well-being.
- That children should be "seen and not heard" and are anchors dragging their parents down.

One can comprise a much longer list of archetype thinking perpetuated by the powers of darkness. These human traditions, philosophies, and prejudices are what must be destroyed (replaced with truth) to free those held captive, enslaved to these conscious and unconscious mindsets.

Part of the work of the saint in doing spiritual warfare is to expose and destroy these philosophies, arguments, and opinions that enslave the mind. That is accomplished by prayer as well as in testimony, witness, and sound teachings.

Destroying these strongholds becomes easier as we ourselves become free of our own archetype mindsets and walk in complete obedience. Complete obedience is accomplished by growing up into Christ, knowing him, embracing all that he taught, and finally being known by him and obeying his voice.

Angel of Light Principalities

Paul made it clear that Satan was involved in deceiving Christians by sending evil human agents into the midst of God's people. The demonic powers behind this scheme can be called *angel of light* principalities.

Satan attempted to destroy Christ; you and I know that failed. Then, in like manner he attempted to destroy the first century church through persecution and martyrdom. That did not work either. So, he began a campaign of infiltration and the institutionalization of Christianity.

Rome makes Christianity its state religion and we see Roman Catholicism take root and begin to suppress Biblical truths and bury the true Gospel in religion. This and other so-called orthodox Christian sects twisted the Gospel to adapt it to the surrounding pagan cultures, making Christianity attractive to pagans by using similar rituals and myths.

These *angel of light* principalities inspired all manner of heresy, disguised with half-truths from Scripture. Those in leadership took on these false teachings in order to compete for souls and keep converts from going back to the pagan cults.

Today, this practice is widespread. Even evangelical denominations allow worldly entertainment and false teachings with pretended signs and wonders to sway and keep converts.

3 - Principalities and Demons

The message of instant change and gold dust falling from the air comes from an *angel of light* principality stemming from the ancient practices of alchemy.

In Paul's letter to the Christians in Corinth he explains the work of Satan appearing as an angel of light to deceive ignorant Christians and how he continually fought to expose them:

"And what I am doing I will continue to do, in order to undermine the claim of those who would like to claim that in their boasted mission they work on the same terms as we do. For such men are false apostles, deceitful workmen, disguising themselves as apostles of Christ. And no wonder, for even Satan disguises himself as an angel of light. So it is no surprise if his servants, also, disguise themselves as servants of righteousness. Their end will correspond to their deeds" (2 Corinthians 11:12-15). (See also Acts 20:29-32, 1 Timothy 4:1-10, 2 Timothy 3:1-9 & 4:1-5 and 2 Thessalonians 2:3-15.)

Ask God to open your eyes to the powerful principalities that control relationships, marriages, church services and many other activities in the community and in fellowship, as well as the world's cultures and the many mounting problems.

As mentioned, the lust for physical and emotional demonstrations of the power of God, similar to the account of Simon the magician in the book of Acts has allowed the devil to appear as an angel of light to empower false anointing bestowed upon false leadership.

Basically there is a high volume marketing campaign going full throttle across much of the Charismatic and Pentecostal forms of Christianity with a focus on selling the anointing and the power of God.

Just as Simon the magician mesmerized the people of Samaria with his magic, God's people are also mesmerized with the practice of false signs and wonders.

Simon became a believer after seeing the true power of God demonstrated by the disciples. And in turn, as a believer he tried to buy from Peter that very power.

Fortunately, Peter saw the issue of Simon's heart and in a straight forward manner he bluntly said, *"May your silver perish with you, because you thought you could obtain the gift of God with money! You have neither part nor lot in this matter, for your heart is not right before God. Repent, therefore, of this wickedness of yours, and pray to the Lord that, if possible, the intent of your heart may be forgiven you. For I see that you are in the gall of bitterness and in the bond of iniquity"* (Acts 8:20-23).

These false signs and wonders by these angel of light principalities are real to an extent—they are false because they give the impression that the miracles were performed by God—they are real because they are supernaturally performed by fallen angels.

Like Simon the magician, many today are not right in their hearts as believers. And like Simon, many lust after the power of God and desire to be glorified like all the other false leaders. Leadership idolatry and lust for God's power is destroying the faith of many and making the Gospel of Christ a object of derision by outsiders who look on in disgust.

False Teachings leading to Carnal Spiritualism

Engaging in true spiritual warfare requires discerning false teachings, counterfeit demonic activity, and carnal spiritualism.

The so called awakenings experienced in the Toronto Blessing movement and other such movements generate

3 - Principalities and Demons

carnal spiritualism. In other terms—an awakening of one's own personal spirit in conjunction with a power demon controlled by an angel of light principality.

These false or empty manifestations follow the same practice of inducement found in a Kundalini awakening that occurs in certain Hindu cults.

Counterfeiting is Satan's favorite work to mislead God's people from sound doctrine and avoid death to carnal spiritualism and death to the works of the flesh. These false teachings help induce *personal spirit driven emotional highs* and become addicting and then easily become a substitute for the true fruit of the Holy Spirit. The fruit of the Holy Spirit should reflect the indwelling presence of God and is maintained within Christians who develop Christ-like character.

These empty manifestations short circuit the work of the cross and sanctification within the believer's life. They are quick-fix lies and false awakenings, but have very real and powerful spiritual and soulish (emotional) sensations.

Churchianity—the Worship of Fellowship

Most churches, especially the high growth mega-churches, have become a physical place to meet and lust after social interactions. Meetings turn into a crowd-induced spiritual feeding frenzy that feeds upon itself. This type of religious crowd spiritualism spawns a carnal spiritualistic dynamic based on relationship networking. A carnal network that undermines growth in Christ, derails mentoring, and fosters shallow fellowship.

Relationship interaction stays shallow with little to no accountability in regard to personal growth, burden bearing, and mentoring. For most, Christian fellowship has become a physical place to get a carnal spiritual buzz once or twice a week that perpetuates the false impression of growth in Christ.

Like the Pharisees' Temple worship system, fellowship becomes a powerful blinding tool used by Satan to keep the majority of God's people alienated from the life God and asleep to the coming hour of visitation. Most Christians stuck in churchianity stay weak and dependent.

Jesus saw how the crowds were accosted, as individuals caught up in the crowd morass, and how they were constantly disheveled—*"harassed and helpless, like sheep without a shepherd"* (Matthew 9:36). Christ's remedy for the crowd chaos was to beseech God to send out laborers to work with those seeking God and help each on an individual basis—and he set this example by limiting his personal work to the group of twelve.

Now in these massive mega-church meetings, the spell of churchianity has made worshiping Christ, the Holy Spirit, and Father God into a perverted system where the act of worship itself becomes an idol and wolves roam freely undetected and unchallenged by leadership.

If churchianity is confronted and called a trap, its crowd dynamic easily turns into gang mentality. (Most proponents of churchianity actually attack true Christians who see through the hype, especially if they preach the uncompromised Gospel of Christ.)

The physical and social church experience (fellowship networking) has developed into relationship addiction and leadership idolatry, and these interactions are infected with carnal spiritualism and hypocrisy. Among other things, this fosters *clique dynamics* that inherently form within the mega-church culture, where a loosely formed

3 - Principalities and Demons

sub-culture within the fellowship grows and gains a powerful controlling influence.

Carnal Christians and wolves in sheep's clothing, often having selfish ambitions to lead, learn how to gain powerful influence within these fellowship cliques. The leaders of these cliques tend to undermine fellowship leadership by imposing an informal authority upon others and healthy body life becomes severely hampered.

In churchianity, gossip, meddling, backbiting, and under handed manipulation take the place of healthy discipleship and mentoring. Preferential attention is given to those who appear to have it together and a subtle indifference is aired towards those who appear to be messed up and in need of serious support.

The truly hurting are often avoided and even subtly shunned. Few dare to become real and honest. Those who desire healing and support get little attention by those who are supposed to be doing the work of ministry. Rather, they are ignored or pushed upon the pastor or an overworked staff.

Churchianity is empowered by a very powerful set of angel of light principalities that require intercessory prayer to break the spell upon individuals trapped in it.

The coming days persecution and extreme birth pangs of the coming kingdom will wake up many from the spell of churchianity, and they will need sound doctrine, mentoring, and prayer to assist in recovering and building up their faith.

Demons
Agents and Workers of the Devil and Fallen Angels

Demons run in the works of the flesh as listed in Galatians 5:19-21, and they blind Christians to inner carnal passions, desires, and impure motives. For example, a familiar demonic spirit of strife can incite quarrels by using hidden bitter jealousies within relationships, whole family systems, and in fellowships.

Until the work of the cross gains access to the inner roots of bitterness, these familiar spirits within family systems will help perpetuate secret sin, abuse, and carnality—deepening hidden ruts of defiling family of origin sins. The demons involved become familiar spirits in the family and will be handed down from generation to generation until they are exposed and secret sins are brought to the light.

Be forewarned, you must patiently endure a demanding personal learning curve. However, this type of training will equip the sincere Christian for spiritual battle with the full armor of God set properly upon Christ-like character.

Demons work within humans and are basically limited to that realm of operation, whereas principalities (fallen angels) work throughout communities, organizations, countries, and regions of the world and employ or direct hordes of demons.

Some theologians believe demons are the spirits of those humans drowned during the great flood. However they may have come into existence, they are part of Satan's minions along with the angels who fell from eternity.

Demons don't like *not having* a resting place and prefer to attach themselves to a human spirit. Familiar spirits associated with sin and works of the flesh will transfer from individual humans known to them or those who fall into defiling, perverted, or otherwise sinful activity.

We are instructed not to hastily lay hands on others that we may not have a demonic transference issue. Also not to keep company with the wicked. Many naïve

3 - Principalities and Demons

Christians without discernment become involved with carnal, defiled, or secret-sin ridden Christians—resulting in being defiled by such.

"Do not be hasty in the laying on of hands, nor take part in the sins of others; keep yourself pure" (1 Timothy 5:22-23).

Do not be deceived: 'Bad company ruins good morals.' Wake up from your drunken stupor, as is right, and do not go on sinning. For some have no knowledge of God. I say this to your shame" (1 Corinthians 15:33-34).

Demons oppress Christians and even possess double minded believers who are laden with defilements and wounds to their personal spirit.

These Christians suffer from past unconfessed sins and a partially seared conscious. Because of the pain of guilt and even from the convicting pain from the Holy Spirit, many wall off the memory of their sins or abuses and pretend these events never happened. They learn to lie to themselves and believe the lie.

Demons latch onto and dwell within these believers and torment to no end. This oppressive torment will continue unless they remember, confess, and repent of the sins in true contrition of heart or receive healing from and resolution of the abuse.

Some turn to false deliverance and get temporary relief only to have the demons return with other demons. This allows the demons to burrow deeper, making the last condition seven times worse (see Matthew 12:43-45).

Many in this condition find relief by unknowingly exchanging tormenting demons for stronger demons of deception. This demonic trade-out has a satanic advantage where stronger demons can use their sin ridden victims more effectively in coordination with counterfeiting angel of light principalities.

Then there are those who have committed a mortal sin, which means that sometime in their past they committed a sin so heinous that death or the death bed will be the only method left that may awaken their conscious to repentance.

The Apostle Paul turned such a person over to death that their spirit might be saved in the day of the Lord. (See 1 Corinthians 5:1-5.) The Apostle John explains in more detail of this kind of condition that people fall into (including believers in Christ): *"If anyone sees his brother committing a sin not leading to death, he shall ask, and God will give him life—to those who commit sins that do not lead to death. There is sin that leads to death; I do not say that one should pray for that. All wrongdoing is sin, but there is sin that does not lead to death"* (1 John 5:16-17).

Ananias and Sapphira died at the hand of the Holy Spirit because they devised a lie to tell Peter about how much they sold a certain piece of property for. These two committed a mortal sin that led to instant judgment, which may very well have spared them eternal damnation. (See Acts 5:1-11.)

Making a Clean Slate and Becoming Religious

Many experience carnal conversions to Christianity and are not truly born again. This condition does not indicate they will never become born of God, but does create a very troubling condition that we call *Gospel Hardened*.

In this condition they make a clean sweep of sin and sinful alliances, only to become self-righteous and lack the required initial inner transformation within their personal spirit by the Spirit of God.

They then try to emulate the attributes of a Christ-like nature in their own efforts by using one of many false teachings that encourage *Christian personality creation*. These become pseudo-Christians, meaning they are not genuine, not authentic, or sincere in spite of outer appearances. These may end up being rejected by Christ, when he says to many false believers, *"I never knew you."*

Many in this condition have demonic strongholds within their character, heart, and/or spirit. The demons may leave initially or later through a so-called deliverance encounter, by a deceived or naïve ministry, only to return later much stronger.

True deliverance comes by becoming born of God through his Spirit, having our personal spirit renewed. Then we learn to work with God in resisting the devil, becoming further cleansed and transformed. This is called sanctification and it is a process that takes time to dissolve the devil's strongholds within one's character. It is also called dying to the works of the flesh and crucifying any and all carnal passions and desires. (See Galatians 5:16-24.)

Double Minded Christians
Crushed in Spirit and Divided in Soul

Many Christians suffer from past trauma, often by being raised in an abusive or dysfunctional home. They become crushed in spirit and double minded (divided in soul). Impurities of heart and spirit easily form within wounded Christians suffering from dividedness of soul, a crushed spirit, and damaged emotions.

For a double minded Christian, demons can harass, torment, oppress, and even cohabitate in dividedness of the soul and within fractured parts of their spirit. Resisting and chasing off the demonic often requires intense effort lasting awhile—where working with the Biblical principles found in the book of James, specifically chapter 3 and 4—eventually brings victory and transformation.

Identifying Demons

When referring to demons, Scripture calls them an unclean spirit, spirits of infirmity, an evil spirit, or spirits of divination, as well as familiar spirits that perpetuate and incites works of the flesh as listed in Galatians.

"Now the works of the flesh are evident: sexual immorality, impurity, sensuality, idolatry, sorcery, enmity, strife, jealousy, fits of anger, rivalries, dissensions, divisions, envy, drunkenness, orgies, and things like these. I warn you, as I warned you before, that those who do such things will not inherit the kingdom of God" (Galatians 5:19-21).

The gifts of the Holy Spirit, with training in the discipline of the Lord, along with proper understanding of God's word, and embracing all that Christ taught, will allow the discerning Christian to ascertain and chase off the demonic in each situation. It is vital that we are able to determine by the Spirit which demons and principalities are in operation upon individuals and which spiritual forces are working in darkness.

Power Demon and Demon of Bliss
Spirit of Sorcery, Spirit of Sensuality and Drunkenness

Again, counterfeiting is Satan's specialty and he is an expert on playing upon naive and immature Christians. Throughout this book we point out Scripture concerning discernment of deception which is a key part in effective spiritual warfare.

3 - Principalities and Demons

As the end-of-this-age approaches, we see all manner of false teachings promoted by false teachers, false prophets, and false apostles. These people claim to know Christ; however, the fruit that follows them spell out wolf.

Over the last thirty years, the negative notoriety of these false teachings, false leaders, and false followers have given a bad name to ministers and to the Gospel of Christ. Peter saw this and warned the following:

"But false prophets also arose among the people, just as there will be false teachers among you, who will secretly bring in destructive heresies, even denying the Master who bought them, bringing upon themselves swift destruction. And many will follow their sensuality, and because of them the way of truth will be blasphemed. And in their greed they will exploit you with false words. Their condemnation from long ago is not idle, and their destruction is not asleep" (2 Peter 2:1-3).

Sensuality, greed, destructive heresies, exploitation, and using false doctrine are now very common and many wolves disguised as Christians are just outright liars. This condition has incited masses of unbelievers and the wicked alike to revile the Gospel of Christ.

Because of the popularity of all these false leaders preaching a false Gospel among deceived Christians, these charlatans continue on and have caused many disrespectful attacks upon Christian leaders and individual Christians. This is a major reason for the increase in persecution.

Tapping into Counterfeit Powers of Darkness

With this end-of-the-age deception, there has arisen a segment of the false who have tapped into Satan's counterfeiting powers. The Apostle Paul also prophesied in his second letter to Timothy that these deceivers would go from bad to worse, walk in a counterfeit faith and practice dark spiritual powers in opposing the truth.

"As Jannes and Jambres opposed Moses, so these men also oppose the truth, men of corrupt mind and counterfeit faith" (2 Timothy 3:8). Jannes and Jambres were the magicians in the Pharaoh's court who held their own against Moses for three plagues, operating in the spiritual powers of darkness.

Today the false wolf has invaded the church of Jesus Christ, just as prophesied in Scripture and practices miracles as did Jannes and Jambres in opposing Moses.

The main types of demons operating with these angel of light ministries are spirits of sorcery and spirits of sensuality and drunkenness.

False manifestations in these false awakenings taking place amongst the Charismatic and Pentecostal are empowered by these spirits. The lust for God's power and the gifts, apart from acquiring them rightly through the discipline and timing of the Lord allows a *power demon* (spirit of sorcery) to enter many.

Further, the craving for inner peace and joy apart from the hard work of the cross acting upon the passions and desires of the flesh, allows counterfeiting *demons of bliss* to enter into the spirits of the deceived believer.

These believers do not walk in the fruit of the Holy Spirit, but in their desire to do so (apart from God's workings) they take a short-cut and learn to tap into their own personal spirit and at the same time invite a demon of bliss to act upon them.

Thus, the extreme-strange manifestations and feelings of ecstasy invading these so-called awakening meetings.

3 - Principalities and Demons

Additionally, false signs and wonders that manifest in these meetings, wrought by the power demons, seem genuine.

Unfortunately, all this leads to Christian sorcery, divination, and false signs and wonders.

Effectively walking in the power of God will require knowing the difference between the power of God and the counterfeiting powers of darkness that hijack the power of the human spirit.

In the coming days true ministers of the Gospel will appear and outshine the false. They will walk in true Pentecostal power and glorify Christ. The difference will become clear, just as the Apostle Paul prophesied about the last days counterfeiters, comparing them to Pharaoh's magicians, *"But they will not get very far, for their folly will be plain to all, as was that of those two men"* (2 Timothy 3:9).

More on the False Awakenings
Hindu Cult Activities Disguised as the Work of the Holy Spirit

As mentioned earlier, the manifestations within these false Pentecostal and Charismatic awakenings and the Hindu sect activities called Kundalini Awakenings are so parallel that anyone with a basic understanding of discernment should see the demonic connection.

Before going into a more detailed comparison and explanation concerning false awakenings in Christianity, it must be made clear that the gifts of the Holy Spirit and the fruit of the Holy Spirit (as explained in Scripture and described in character by Biblical accounts) were never meant to cease!

Our ministry works within the Biblical guidelines for practicing the gifts of the Holy Spirit and applying sound doctrine to help each disciple to grow in the grace and discipline of the Lord.

That chastising discipline, training, and Holy Spirit leadership produces death to the works of our old nature. This hard work allows the Holy Spirit to bring the resurrected life, bearing the fruit of the Holy Spirit within our inner being.

Counterfeit Inner Being Nirvana
Avoiding the Chastising Work of the Holy Spirit

One of the works of the Holy Spirit explained by the Apostle Paul in his letter to the Christians in Galatia is how the Holy Spirit opposes (is in conflict) with the desires of the flesh. (Read carefully Galatians 5:16-26.)

The conflict between the Holy Spirit's presence within us and our carnal desires and passions is ongoing and often unpleasant. Within ourselves we will experience conflicting thoughts, temptations, and emotional outbursts—having moments that lack peace, often bothered with anxieties, feelings of oppression, and sometimes deep depression. These are some symptoms of this ongoing conflict.

This is part of the normal processes of having the Holy Spirit make known to us the often invisible issues of heart and defilements of spirit that still lurk within us (after we are born again).

However, false doctrine that states that all bad thoughts, impurities of heart, and defilements within the spirit are miraculously (magically) removed when we are born again creates a giant theological contradiction.

Satan's angel of light scheme is to alleviate this contradiction and perpetuate false doctrine by offering the

3 - Principalities and Demons

counterfeit fruit of the Holy Spirit. The counterfeiting work of the devil is to deceive Christians in such a way as to by-pass the dying-to-self work of the cross. The discipline of the Lord and the Holy Spirit's inner cleansing and sanctifying work is being all-out subverted.

This is one major reason for the insurgence of false teachers inspired by the demonic. The false awakening movements offer a magic touch from heaven to quell the inner conflicts and achieve inner Christian nirvana—instantly without any discomfort.

Nirvana defined: Spiritual enlightenment, state of grace, bliss, joy, pleasure, paradise, heaven.

Releasing the Awakening Snake
Inviting Demonic Control of the Human Spirit

Many today warn of the counterfeiting activity within these Christian awakening movements, but few explain specifically how the demonic slithers in, to take the place of the Holy Spirit.

Jessie Penn-Lewis, in her book War on the Saints (unabridged version) explains some of the methods and reasons the 1904-05 Welch revival was hijacked by the devil through false leadership and empty manifestations. Later, she and other discerning saints warned of the Eastern Mysticism creeping into western cultures and into Christianity, specifically Hindu cult practices.

For the discerning saint, just a little research will bring to light Satan's work within the false revivals and false awakenings so wide spread within the church today.

These false movements have gone from the fringes of Christianity to main stream church popularity since the 1904-05 Wales revival and radically oppose New

Testament guidelines and doctrines for fellowship. The counterfeiting activity has grown to a ground swell movement deceiving millions of believers into inviting the associated demons to take control of their personal spirits.

The demonic enter by invitation and by transference from leaders, and these encounters result in the partial possession of the human spirit.

Symptoms are obvious; uncontrolled spasms, shaking, delusions, spontaneous convulsions, emotional episodes, and strange sensations of euphoria.

Simply explained, the demons enter with minimal natural resistance from the victim's personal spirit (because of deception, passivity, and acquiesce to total submission with no discernment). To the deceived believer it's the Holy Spirit entering their personal spirit.

Mild Symptoms of Possession
An Insidious Strategy that Leads to Cohabitation

Satan and the demonic do not want to blow their cover by bouncing their victims around too much. Thus, the euphoric feelings, gentle falling down, mild twitching and jerking, along with the false gifting is demonically designed to quell any misgivings—fun spiritual manifestations all controlled to dig a deeper hole within the human spirit in order to set up cohabitation.

Otherwise, if the true intent was expressed by the demonic up front, those counterfeit empty manifestations would be more like the following:

"And behold, a man from the crowd cried out, 'Teacher, I beg you to look at my son, for he is my only child. And behold, a spirit seizes him, and he suddenly cries out. It convulses him so that he foams at the mouth, and shatters him, and will hardly

3 - Principalities and Demons

leave him. And I begged your disciples to cast it out, but they could not.' Jesus answered, 'O faithless and twisted generation, how long am I to be with you and bear with you? Bring your son here.' While he was coming, the demon threw him to the ground and convulsed him. But Jesus rebuked the unclean spirit and healed the boy, and gave him back to his father. And all were astonished at the majesty of God" (Luke 9:38-43).

The following testimony is from a deceived non-Christian who has experienced a Kundalini awakening. Her testimony is taken from her blog. Compare her description to the testimony of so many caught up in the false awakenings.

> "Nine years ago, I had a Spontaneous Kundalini Rising. It rose to my Sacral Chakra and for two months, I had the most intense Kundalini activity of my life (so far!). I had very strong stomach contractions that would lift my upper body off the bed. I had spontaneous Orgasms and moments of complete bliss. When my Kundalini was most intense, I began speaking and singing in a language that I did not know. I guess you can say I was speaking in tongues. I also would go into trance like states at random times. Mostly when I relaxed or went to bed. Most of this activity was strongest at bed time and still continues to do so.
>
> When this all happened, I had no clue what was happening to me. I never felt an evil or oppressive presence. I knew this was of an obvious spiritual nature. I was a spiritual person before this happened and I meditated every once in a while. I did not have a structured spiritual practice."

Gwen Mims blog February 7, 2014

The following is Gwen Mims profile from her blog:

> Hello!
> Life is journey and I am an eager seeker of Knowledge, Truth, and Enlightenment.
> I currently reside in the South Eastern United States. I am single and live with my four furry feline angels. I am blessed to have my loving and supportive friends and family.
> In 2002 began my Kundalini Awakening Journey. Its been an terrifying and amazing experience. Unable to afford a Guru or Spiritual Teacher, I have used my gut instinct while trying to listen to my Kundalini for answers. I have learned a lot about myself and I am a lot more stronger than I ever realized.
> On January 20, 2013, My Kundalini rose to my Throat Chakra. With it, comes a new chapter in my Spiritual Journey.
> I have been a Solitary Wiccan for Twenty Five Years. Part of my journey is to become closer to my Goddess.
> I recently started a Blog that I hope will help others who had a Spontaneous Kundalini Awakening. It's a mix of facts and my own personal experiences with Kundalini. What has worked for me and what hasn't.

The following are Kundalini Awakening physical and psychological side effects. These side effects are almost identical to Christians we have mentored and counseled who come away for these false awakenings.

Some of these symptoms are experienced by Christians doing spiritual warfare or who are be attacked by people practicing sorcery.

3 - Principalities and Demons

Those studying Kundalini awakenings believe these physical effects are a sign of a Kundalini awakening and some researchers describe them as unwanted side effects.

- Involuntary jerks, tremors, shaking, itching, tingling, and crawling sensations, especially in the arms and legs.
- Energy rushes or feelings of electricity circulating the body
- Intense heat (sweating) or cold.
- Spontaneous breathing, motionless and semi-frozen state.
- Visions or sounds at times associated with a particular part(s) of the body.
- Diminished or conversely extreme sexual desire sometimes leading to a state of constant or whole-body orgasm.
- Emotional upheavals or surfacing of unwanted and repressed feelings or thoughts with certain repressed emotions becoming dominant in the conscious mind for short or long periods of time.
- Headache, migraine, or pressure inside the skull.
- Increased blood pressure and irregular heartbeat.
- Emotional numbness.
- Antisocial tendencies.
- Mood swings with periods of depression or mania.
- Pains in different areas of the body, especially back and neck.
- Sensitivity to light, sound, and touch.
- Trance-like and altered states of consciousness.
- Disrupted sleep pattern (periods of insomnia or oversleeping).
- Loss of appetite or overeating.
- Bliss, feelings of infinite love and universal connectivity, transcendent awareness.

The symptoms of the false manifestations are widespread and serious and indicate a massive invasion of the demonic in certain streams of Christianity, particularly in the Charismatic, Pentecostal, and many Evangelical fellowships. Indeed, as forewarned in scripture:

"Therefore, rejoice, O heavens and you who dwell in them! But woe to you, O earth and sea, for the devil has come down to you in great wrath, because he knows that his time is short!" (Revelation 12:12).

Extraterrestrials — Demonic Physical Manifestations
Another Insidious Deception of the Devil

Movies, books, eyewitness accounts of UFOs, abductions by alien life, and scientific search to contact ET have grown exponentially. The Star Wars movies and books, along with Star Trek have created cult followings, and now anyone can download software from SETI. A scientific experiment called SETI@home, which uses Internet-connected computers in the Search for Extraterrestrial Intelligence (SETI), requires installation of a free program that downloads and analyzes radio telescope data.

E.T. and alien images are very common now. What was once considered hideous demonic beasts are now thought of as extraterrestrial intelligent life that can possibly help the world overcome its many problems.

The movie E.T. helped children of all ages and adults accept the existence of life from outer space as friendly, superior in power, and more intelligent than humans.

In November 2009 the Vatican hosted a five day conference of scientists from around the world to study the possibility of alien life.

José Funes, a Jesuit priest, helped coordinate the conference. As a Vatican representative on this research he

3 - Principalities and Demons

said, "How can we rule out that life may have developed elsewhere? Just as there is a multitude of creatures on Earth, there could be other beings, even intelligent ones, created by God. This does not contradict our faith, because we cannot put limits on God's creative freedom."

Many Protestant Christians believe the same thing and a multitude of Christians have enjoyed Hollywood's entertaining movies, such as Star Trek, Star Wars, and E.T. as well as dozens of other alien movies and books.

These images of aliens and extraterrestrials are satanically inspired caricatures of demons. Billions of people of all nations, including millions upon millions of Christians, gaze at these hideous images, unknowingly and indirectly worshiping demons. Like stooges, Christians are being subtly programmed to accept the rise of the Beast as an E.T. and worship it!

The possibility of Satan deceiving the whole world, including multitudes of Christians, by having a fallen angel physically appearing as an extraterrestrial life form with great power and superior intelligence is not far-fetched.

Indeed, Apostle John, if viewing one of the modern day movie images of an E.T. would certainly describe it as a "beast."

Does Scripture clarify that aliens exist? In Jude it states, *"And the angels that did not keep their own position <u>but left their proper dwelling</u> have been kept by him in eternal chains in the nether gloom until the judgment of the great day"* (Jude 1:6). A third of the angels rebelled and sided with Lucifer and left their proper dwelling in the heavens to help deceive and set up rule on earth.

As true believers, we are to understand all the schemes of Satan so we may not be caught off guard; having the

"Beast" of Revelation appear as a brilliant and powerful extraterrestrial, coming to earth to help, and with signs and wonders so convincing as to possibly deceived the most discerning saint. (See 2 Thessalonians 2:9-12.)

As it is now many Christians caught up in the false movements have unknowingly and voluntarily made it easy for the demonic to reside within their beings—happily and unhampered.

Chapter 4

Evil, the Human Spirit, and Co-Habitation

An Evil World Getting More Evil

Whether we want to accept the truth or not, the fact is we live in a very evil world. The end of World War II did not eradicate mass evils. Mass murders by one race or religion against another have become worse, beyond comprehension. Now evil is on the verge of engulfing the whole world in terrible troubles. Jesus said of this coming evil, *"For then there will be great tribulation, such as has not been from the beginning of the world until now, no, and never will be. And if those days had not been cut short, no human being would be saved"* (Matthew 24:21-22).

This chapter will not tackle the whole subject of evil and the coming evils that will consume the whole world in war and mass brutality. We will focus on what Christ taught and how He defined evil in relation to Satan's character and influences toward human evil as described in attitude and behavior in day-to-day living.

Evil is alive and thriving everywhere; the next-door neighbor who you thought you knew, a homeless street person acting strange, a pedophile running a local daycare, a beloved high school student who for no apparent reason goes on a killing spree.

Unexplained hatred of a person of one race towards another race, hatred of the Jews, the various genocides in Africa, the list is virtually endless. Understanding evil is impossible apart from the Bible's explanation and Christ's teachings. Once we understand evil's true nature and its agenda, the only hope of overcoming evil and the final eradication of evil comes from Scripture and in the second coming of Christ.

Breaking Denial

Christians who maintain a "Pollyanna" denial concerning the existence of evil will soon have their imaginary world-view shattered. Those who continue to play the positive thinking "glad game" in life will not withstand the coming rise of evil.

We must embrace the true biblical world-view concerning evil and it's remedy in order to successfully navigate in the coming dark days—because the days are evil and evil will become over-the-top, touching everyone. For a short season, the devil and evil will have dominion over the whole world. Suffering and calamities will become unprecedented—for the devil and his angels are in the process of being kicked out of heaven and thrown down to the earth. *"Woe to you, O earth and sea, for the devil has come down to you in great wrath, because he knows that his time is short!"* (Revelation 12:12). A literal hell on earth will prevail until Christ returns.

Those who believe they are exempt from the coming unleashed powers of evil are sadly mistaken; soon the lost, the unprepared, and self-righteous Christians alike will cry like Job due to the extreme evils about to befall them. Those who wake up, deal with their denial, and pay the price to stand in the coming flood of evils will glorify God, endure to the end, and overcome in Christ.

Theology that teaches a cure or healing for human evil is an outright lie—a satanic lie. Ministries and Christian

4 - Evil, the Human Spirit, and Co-Habitation

workers who are naïve in these matters will be in for the shock of their lives. It is through evil people that the devil performs his most terrible work. If we bury our heads in the sand, look the other way, and pretend that we will be magically insulated from the powers of hell and the work of evil, then we can expect extra and unnecessary misery.

The Apostle Paul laid out a powerful guide on avoiding evil and overcoming the devil's works: *"<u>Take note of those</u> who create dissensions and difficulties, in opposition to the doctrine which you have been taught; avoid them. For such persons do not serve our Lord Christ, but their own appetites, and <u>by fair and flattering words they deceive the hearts of the simple-minded</u>* [naïve]. *For while your obedience is known to all, so that I rejoice over you, I would have you <u>wise as to what is good and guileless</u>* [no longer deceived] *as to what is evil; then the God of peace will <u>soon crush Satan under your feet</u>"* (Romans 16:17-20 RSV).

We must learn to be aware of evil, be alert, and abide in the true Christ—we must allow the Spirit to lead in all things and learn what is pleasing to the Lord. The days are becoming dark and full of evil because Satan has an army of servants who have sold out to evil. *"Look carefully then how you walk, not as unwise but as wise, making the best use of the time, because the days are evil. Therefore do not be foolish, but understand what the will of the Lord is"* (Ephesians 5:15-17).

The Hour of Evil and the Power of Darkness
A Time in Every Disciple's Life Where Discernment Is Perfected

The righteous in charge of the Temple worship system got away with murder—the murder of our Lord. Imagine the disciples' reaction and the emotions that filled their hearts when the Temple leaders came to arrest Jesus. They were prepared to fight; in fact, Peter drew his sword and cut off an ear of one of the arresting guards.

Jesus stopped Peter and the others, healed the ear of the wounded servant, and then said to the chief priests and the others that came to arrest him, *"Have you come out as against a robber, with swords and clubs? When I was with you day after day in the temple, you did not lay hands on me. <u>But this is your hour, and the power of darkness</u>"* (Luke 22:52-53).

As we discuss evil and its reality, it is important to understand that Christ will allow his sincere servants to endure a time when evil will prevail in their lives and in their ministry. When we are ready, Christ will lead us through a time of defeat, just as he allowed the apostles to suffer humiliation and asked them to submit to the powers of darkness and not to fight it.

Until we taste the power of evil and its treachery and reel from evil's surreal and deadly force, we will always be under its shadow and threat. In addition, I must add, staying ignorant and hiding will not excuse us from the last-days evil invading our culture and the world—no one will be exempt. *"For it will come upon all who dwell on the face of the whole earth. But stay awake at all times, praying that you may have strength to escape all these things that are going to take place, and to stand before the Son of Man."* (Luke 21:35-36).

Reading and studying are vital. We must learn and embrace all that Christ taught and we must understand that he will perform the same kind of training that he arranged for the Apostles.

When we break denial concerning evil (especially evil that appears good) and understand how easily evil can work in the power of darkness, then we must endure it personally. Suffering at the hands of evil after we have learned of it drives

4 - Evil, the Human Spirit, and Co-Habitation

the lessons home and trains us to avoid and deal with evil God's way. Jesus taught the disciples about evil in detail, and repeatedly; however, not until they endured the powers of darkness did they know and understand.

Jesus still teaches his disciples, and then trains them in all aspects of living in a dark, evil, and dangerous world. Then and only then will our hearts no longer be deceived by evil's lies and its flatteries, and our naïveté will turn to wisdom. *"Behold, I am sending you out as sheep in the midst of wolves, so be wise as serpents and innocent as doves"* (Matthew 10:16).

The Apostle Paul sheds more light on those times when all seems lost and the powers of darkness prevail. He wrote, *"For we do not want you to be ignorant, brothers, of the affliction we experienced in Asia. For we were so utterly burdened beyond our strength that we despaired of life itself. Indeed, we felt that we had received the sentence of death. But <u>that was to make us rely not on ourselves but on God who raises the dead</u>. He delivered us from such a deadly peril, and he will deliver us. On him we have set our hope that he will deliver us again"* (2 Corinthians 1:8-10).

Quite candidly, most Christians learn to rely on their own strength and clouded wisdom and in their immaturity try to deal with evil and attempt to expose darkness. (If Jesus had allowed Peter and the other disciples to fight against his arrest, all would have been lost.)

Dear friend, if you are serious about God using you mightily in the coming days, then brace for an hour of suffering when evil seems to win and the powers of darkness run roughshod over certain areas of your life and ministry. The disciples were not arrested with Christ, but they did hide from the wicked until that hour of evil passed.

Fighting the Evil Human Spirit

This battle is the most difficult to explain, and perhaps the most potent in Satan's arsenal. Most Christians are completely unaware of this spiritual threat. The potential power of the *unregenerate* personal spirit of a human being can be lethal. A great misunderstanding exists within the body of Christ concerning the nature of our personal spirit.

We, as humans, have a personal spirit. It is that part of us that is alive and invisible, yet held in place within the human physical body. If the human spirit departs from the body, the body dies.

Some might be aware of the New Age books written by Shirley Maclaine or other writers on the subject of the spiritual power of mankind. Simply put, these deceived people stumbled onto (by satanic influence) the power of the human spirit.

They developed demonic-inspired methods to help induce astral projection of their own spirit (human spirit travel). That is, they develop the ability to send their inner person (or spirit) out of the body to travel to other places. Demonic spirits intertwined with their human spirit provide the spiritual power. These deceived people crave power. And by embracing new age or eastern mysticism, their personal spirit becomes connected to a *power demon,* which helps their personal spirit temporarily leave their body.

Similar teachings have even infiltrated parts of the charismatic movement as these wayward teachers cite Paul's statement in 1 Corinthians 5:3-5, *"For though absent in body I am present in spirit, and as if present, I have already pronounced judgment in the name of the Lord Jesus on the man who has done such a thing. When you are assembled, and my spirit is present, with the power of our Lord Jesus, you are to*

4 - Evil, the Human Spirit, and Co-Habitation

deliver this man to Satan for the destruction of the flesh, that his spirit may be saved in the day of the Lord Jesus."

If indeed, Paul's personal spirit was out of body, it was in the power of the Holy Spirit, not in his willful choice with demonic assistance.

The teaching of Catholicism calls this spiritual activity "bilocation" and it is defined as follows:

Bilocation. Multiple or simultaneous presence of the same substance of soul in two places distant from each other. Bilocations have been frequently reported in the lives of the saints. (*Modern Catholic Dictionary*, by John A. Hardon, S.J. Doubleday & Company, Inc., 1980. Page 67).

Occult practice makes astral projection a fundamental goal for beginners, a rudimentary aspect of witchcraft or sorcery. This is a particular aspect of the satanic spirit world activity that allows a demonic force to enlist a human spirit to attack another person or another Christian. This is done with or without the knowledge of the person whose personal spirit is being enlisted in this kind of spiritual attack.

Satan and demons can enlist human spirits virtually at will, due to the many doorways that Christians and non-Christians have created and allowed to stay within their spirit.

Doorways are defilements to our spirit from exposure to occult practices and teachings. The following practices are what many fall into: necromancy, the Ouija board, psychic readings, palm readings, movies depicting sorcery (the TV series, *Bewitched*, was a powerful doorway exposing millions of adults and children to sorcery), self-hypnotism and childhood abuses to name a few.

The *Harry Potter* books and movies have defiled and lured millions of children worldwide into occult practices, sorcery, and spiritualism. Satan's plans have become bold, taking masses of children into darkness. Christ warned of those who would cause little ones to stumble—that instant execution would be a light sentence. God will hold these authors, actors, and others who promote such evils as *Bewitched, Harry Potter, The Wizard of Oz, and so many more that could be listed,* accountable. (See Matthew 18:6-9).

Unresolved anger and lack of forgiveness embedded within the heart and spirit of a person is another tool that Satan can use to gain access to and use a human spirit, especially when coupled with the aforementioned doorways. As it says in Scripture, these things give opportunity to Satan. (See Ephesians 4:25-31).

Note: *We have found that adults who suffered molestation in childhood can have multiple satanic doorways. Often defilements forced victims to suppress, repress and in many cases instantly dissociate from the pain and perversion created by these abuses. Proper emotional response and cries for help were also buried in like manner. The sun went down many times on the associated shame and anger along with other damaged emotions. These incidents indeed give Satan an opportunity to gain access to the abused child's spirit. As born-again adult Christians we can have many of these wounds, defilements, and doorways are lodged deep within, waiting like time bombs to be satanically ignited. Very significant symptoms like dreams where one is flying in the air indicate a doorway that must be closed. The Holy Spirit should be allowed the freedom in healthy fellowship to expose these hidden wounds. Each local body of believers should be trained to help facilitate support and recovery that will effectively foster cleansing, healing, and wholeness.*

When Christians battle evil, often Satan will attempt to enlist a human spirit in his scheme of attack and

4 - Evil, the Human Spirit, and Co-Habitation

counterattacks. Many Christians have unhealthy relationships with people who have not cleansed themselves of such defilements. These defilements are what allow the intertwining of the demonic with the human spirit.

Often Christians doing warfare are unaware of their own defilements that can also make battles more intense and more dangerous. True Christians who find themselves in this type of warfare must look to their own issues that will magnify these curse-filled attacks.

Many Christians give cause for these attacks to take affect due to their own defilements not yet exposed and cleansed. *"Like a sparrow in its flitting, like a swallow in its flying, a curse that is causeless does not alight"* (Proverbs 26:2).

Jesus warned us concerning hidden or harbored issues of heart such as unforgiveness and revenge. Millions of Christians have hearts loaded down with issues of jealousy, hate, unforgiveness, and sin. All this allows Satan and demons to inspire curses and spiritual oppression leading these defiled and wounded Christians to attack each other spiritually. Many fellowships struggle with all manner of disorder and vile practices. These double-minded carnal Christians spew poison almost every time they open their mouths.

"But no human being can tame the tongue—a restless evil, full of deadly poison. With it we bless the Lord and Father, and with it we curse men, who are made in the likeness of God. From the same mouth come blessing and cursing. My brethren, this ought not to be so. Does a spring pour forth from the same opening fresh water and brackish? Can a fig tree, my brethren, yield olives, or a grapevine figs? No more can salt water yield fresh. Who is wise and understanding among you? By his good life let him show his works in the meekness of wisdom. But if you

have bitter jealousy and selfish ambition in your hearts, do not boast and be false to the truth. This wisdom is not such as comes down from above, but is earthly, unspiritual, devilish. For where jealousy and selfish ambition exist, there will be disorder and every vile practice" (James 3:8-16).

Satan will drive this condition to its maximum effectiveness, using defiled human spirits against each other. Indeed, as James put it, out of the double-minded Christian flows blessing and curses, clean and foul water. This causes trouble, sickness, strange events and all manner of evil situations.

The unclean human spirit of the lost and the sinful double-minded Christian can incite common symptoms of severe headaches, nausea, and extreme loss of energy. In more extreme cases, symptoms of such attacks may include severe physical pain, near fatal accidents and overwhelming oppression. Often sickness and severe illness manifest themselves by the continued spiritual attack upon the immune system and cause prolonged high blood pressure. The following quote from *Soul and Spirit* by Jessie Penn-Lewis will point out some symptoms of this kind of spiritual attack. Penn-Lewis referred to this power as *soul or psychic power* as rather than *human spirit power*.

"How this ignorant bringing into action of psychic force can affect spiritual believers has come to me in a recent letter. The writer says, 'I have just come through a terrible onslaught of the enemy. Hemorrhage, heart affection, panting and exhaustion. My whole body in a state of collapse. It suddenly burst upon me while at prayer to pray against all psychic power exercised upon me by (psychic) 'prayer'. By faith in the power of the Blood of Christ, I cut myself off from it, and the result was remarkable. Instantly my breathing became normal, the hemorrhage stopped,

4 - Evil, the Human Spirit, and Co-Habitation

exhaustion vanished, all pain fled, and life came back to my body. I have been refreshed and invigorated ever since. God let me know in confirmation of this deliverance, that my condition was the effect of a group of deceived souls who are in opposition to me 'praying' about me! God has used me to the deliverance of two of them, but the rest are in an awful pit.'" (*Soul and Spirit*, Jessie Penn-Lewis, Christian Literature Crusade, 1989 page 58).

A more modern description of this spiritual power is that Satan harnesses the unregenerate human spirit or the divided portion of the personal spirit of the double-minded Christian. The devil can capture and channel inroads through the human soul (mind and emotions) into the personal spirit by years of grooming and inciting forbidden practices. This condition can progress to demonic possession and possibly demonic infestation-cohabitation.

God's desire is to be in communion with true Christians through their regenerated spirit. God's plan is to regenerate the human spirit and separate the regenerated spirit from the soulish and carnal influence, as well as the demonic influences, by way of rebirth, cleansing, and sanctification in conjunction with the work of the cross.

I can attest to this type of demonic-human spirit power. When hit by this power, you will know firsthand its serious effect and murderous potential. Passivity or disassociation is symptomatic of oppressed and possessed humans, as well as demon-infested or double-minded Christians. This passivity is a disconnect from the physical or life's realities and is characterized by a lack of empathy and/or a seared conscience.

Yes, this is Satan's most insidious war plan: to enlist human spirits who have become zombie-like agents of satanic principalities—those world rulers of this present darkness.

Paul wrote to Timothy; *"Do not be hasty in the laying on of hands, nor participate in another man's sins; keep yourself pure"* (1 Timothy 5:22). There can be transference of familiar and defiling spirits, as well as hidden jealousy and hatreds directed by these types of people against Christians and by double-minded Christians against each other. You can be sure that Satan will drum up this type of person once a Christian makes a stand to do true spiritual warfare.

When fighting this, the disciple must understand that the human spirit, coupled with the demonic spirit, has additional power to inflict spiritual, emotional, physical, and even severe illness or death upon their targeted victims.

We must understand this aspect of Satan's work. Further, we must learn to mitigate these attacks by becoming pure in heart and cleansed of all defilements of body and spirit to gain victory in this type of spiritual warfare.

"Since we have these promises, beloved, let us cleanse ourselves from every defilement of body and spirit, bringing holiness to completion in the fear of God" (2 Corinthians 7:1).

Rebuking the demonic in the name of Jesus is part of the battle, and also we must learn how to discern if a human spirit might be an accomplice in the attack.

The human spirit has free will; therefore, one must work with the Holy Spirit to reject a human spirit attack by invoking a prayer that states, "The Lord rebuke you!" Often the battle to ward off such attacks may take days where intermittent one or two hour prayer sessions take place.

4 - Evil, the Human Spirit, and Co-Habitation

As one grows in the Christ-like character, fighting off or warding off a human spirit attack becomes easier as the power of God's might flows unhindered.

Another important aspect in fighting an evil human spirit is to identify the human spirit involved. Here the gifts of the Holy Spirit are vital—especially prophecy, words of wisdom, words of discernment and words of knowledge concerning the invisible works of Satan against the saint.

Examining the ties between you and the person(s) who are in spiritual conflict against you will help bring insight and understanding. You may need to tactfully break off the relationship. Pray for the exposure of their hidden agenda then confront them, and above all, hold no resentment or revenge against them.

Forgiveness is an important key for victory in these cases. The reason Satan snares so many in this scheme stems from unresolved anger, unforgiveness, and bitter jealousy. A reminder; *a curse without cause will not take hold*—if we have our own issues of unforgiveness and bitterness (a cause), these issues can allow a curse to take hold.

The best approach is to avoid such people. The Lord may require you to pray that the person facilitating these attacks have their eyes opened to the Gospel. In some cases, turning them over to judgment may be required. (See 1 Corinthians 5:1-5 and 1 Timothy 1:18-20).

There is one last but very important concern to express on this subject. Satan uses many Christians in this manner because they have never embraced the cross. They maintain a carnal state of *being* and often carry defilements of soul and spirit wherever they go. Their spirit and soul are intertwined, and this condition can cause demonic infestation if they are divided or double-minded.

Again, *double-minded* Christian is the term used concerning this critical area of spiritual warfare. These Christians can be very dangerous to work with, confront, and support.

Studying the book of James will lay out the characteristics and symptoms of these unstable Christians whom Satan often enlists in his most brutal spiritual attacks.

And with the increased exposure to the practices of witchcraft throughout the American culture, the human spirits of multitudes are now subject to the solicitation and use by the demonic.

Last Days Sorcery
Satanic Hijacking of the Human Spirit

Satan is working hard to capture and harness the human spirit to assist in attacking God's people and to promote man's will. Many suffer spiritual defilements from exposure to witchcraft and other forbidden practices, and amazingly many Christians have unknowingly opened spiritual doorways that allow them to channel for the devil.

Scripture foretells of a coming end-of-this-age chaos where sorcery becomes a major weapon employed by the devil and evil people, false believers, and even carnal Christians.

The harnessing of the human spirit is a significant part of the devil's work, which is now unfolding and will be arrayed against God's people on many fronts. It will become manifest within fellowships through carnal Christians deceived by false doctrine and practicing counterfeit gifts.

4 - Evil, the Human Spirit, and Co-Habitation

Satan will be allowed to use evil people in society such as new age practitioners as well as cult and occult practitioners who hate God and hate Christians. Moreover, Christians will be attacked by any means, where the demonic can enlist and power boost the human spirit to oppose God's will and the work of the pure and true body of Christ.

Satan is very much into harnessing this last-day's magic-and-sorcery-soaked generation. Many today are drenched in these abominable portrayals of supernatural magic. Then they become believers in Christ, like Simon the magician. Yet they are not confronted concerning their magic thinking like Peter confronted Simon.

Few learn how to purify their hearts and become healed of their bitter jealousies, and be set free from the enthrallment of magic they ingested into their carnal nature (which is still defiled even after they believe in Christ) from living in a magic-laden culture.

In days to come this type of demonic channeling through deceived carnal Christians will become acute, with the demonic assaulting fellowships by inciting Christians to turn on each other spiritually.

A Christian witchcraft mêlée will develop in many congregations that have embraced these false doctrines and fostered false manifestations. Any hidden bitter jealousy or selfish ambition within deceived and defiled Christians will boost the power of the human spirit through counterfeit power demons thought to be the Holy Spirit.

Again, illnesses, accidents, mishaps, even premature death, along with weird and chaotic circumstances will become out of hand, as many fellowships experience a satanically induced internal meltdown. Few pastors will understand what is happening and how this kind of spiritual attack on so many grew so quickly. Prayer against such will do little to stop this coming attack.

Walking in the fullness of Christ and having the full armor of God properly worn in Christ-like character will be the only safe course to follow. Those who overcome and endure the discipline of the Lord in his training will be victorious and stand in the evil day.

Demonic Cohabitation

Few understand the goal of Satan and the demonic concerning demon possession or how Satan deceives in order to gain a friendly place of residence within the human spirit that spills into the soul (emotions and mind).

As mentioned earlier, the work of the devil in the last days is to gain entrance into the very core of human beings and deceive from within through pagan practices, defiling sins, and false teachings in Christianity.

Most of the mentally ill suffer from the effects of a crushed spirit and dividedness of soul, along with demonic cohabitation. Most labeled as mentally ill demonstrate the negative side of demonic cohabitation where the demonic are more destructive and tormenting—rather than being more benign in the symptoms of cohabitation as with many who are deceived within the many Christian false manifestations movements or who are friendly cohabitating partners in pagan and cult practices.

Satan easily filled the heart of Judas so as to use him to betray Christ, because Judas had a devilish nature from the beginning. (See John 6:70-71.)

However, after the devil was finished with Judas, we see cohabitation with the devil turn into the characteristics

4 - Evil, the Human Spirit, and Co-Habitation

of a demonically possessed person, leaving Judas to extreme torment that drove him to suicide.

Discernment and the fullness of Christ, while warring in the power of God's might will be the only road to victory for the sincere Christian in the coming days.

Chapter 5

Finger of God Power and Prayer

Jesus cast out a mute demon and then the man spoke and the people who saw this marveled, however, *"Some of them said, 'He casts out demons by Beelzebul, the prince of demons,'"* (Luke 11:15).

In a portion of our Lord's response he states, *"And if I cast out demons by Beelzebul, by whom do your sons cast them out? Therefore they will be your judges. But if it is by the finger of God that I cast out demons, then the kingdom of God has come upon you"* (Luke 11:19-20).

If Christ cast out demons by the power available in just one of God's fingers, then by what power did the sons of Israel (Jewish exorcists) cast them out? If not by Beelzebul (the devil) nor by the power of God, then by whom did they cast demons?

We see this kind of successful deliverance activity in many pagan rituals. And Jesus said that many Christians would do mighty works in his name, including prophesying and casting out demons. It was certainly not in the power of Christ or by the Holy Spirit, since Jesus referred to these Christians as being lawless and not known by Christ.

Nor was God working through the Jewish sons, and God certainly does not work through pagans.

So by what power do false Christians, the Jewish exorcists, and pagan witchdoctors perform exorcisms?

The human spirit through religious rituals can amass enough spiritual energy whereby demons will often have to leave their possessed victims (at least temporarily). The *supernatural feats of power* in these exorcism are performed by the power of the human spirit.

Many Christians today practice supernatural feats using human spirit power, which is often boosted by the power of a counterfeiting demon.

A spirit of divination, masquerading as the Holy Spirit can counterfeit the gift of prophesy or a word of knowledge.

Millions of Charismatic and Pentecostal Christians practice a prayer language in the power of their own personal spirit. A power demon can disguise itself as the gift of tongues and inspire naïve-carnal Christians to develop a false tongue within their personal spirit.

Few Christians practice discernment or know how to test the spirits.

"Beloved, do not believe every spirit, but test the spirits to see whether they are from God, for many false prophets have gone out into the world" (1 John 4:1).

In the Power of His Might
Exorcism, Deliverance and Healing—by the Finger of God

When a sincere disciple of Christ endures the Lord's training and discipline, they will have succeeded in working through the cleansing fires of sanctification.

Then, like the original disciples, they will walk in the true authority of Christ's name and are able to cast out demons, heal the sick, expose darkness, and confront evil people and imposters—in the true power of Christ (Christ working through them).

Unfortunately, many leaders and Christian workers today walk in a counterfeit faith where empty manifestations and false deliverances are the norm.

They develop the spiritual power of the human spirit often boosted by counterfeiting demonic spirits.

As a reminder, Jesus warned, *"Not everyone who says to me, 'Lord, Lord,' shall enter the kingdom of heaven, but he who does the will of my Father who is in heaven. On that day many will say to me, 'Lord, Lord, <u>did we not prophesy in your name, and cast out demons in your name, and do many mighty works in your name</u>?' And then will I declare to them, '<u>I never knew you; depart from me, you evildoers</u>'"* (Matthew 7:21-23).

The Need for True Leadership and Mature Workers

Christ warned that in the last days of this age there would arise many false leaders who ensnare Christians away from following Christ, to follow after them. False leaders and leadership who are confused, divisive, competitive, false, and self-styled are the main compelling reasons why so many of God's people are amiss with their relationship with God—true leadership will ensure God's people develop a true relationship with Christ.

The Apostle Paul exhorts, *"For I did not shrink from declaring to you the whole counsel of God. Pay careful attention to yourselves and to all the flock, in which the Holy Spirit has made you overseers, to care for the church of God, which he obtained with his own blood. I know that after my departure fierce wolves will come in among you, not sparing the flock; and from among your own selves will arise men speaking twisted things, to draw away the disciples after them. Therefore be alert, remembering that for three years I did not cease night or day to admonish every one with tears"* (Acts 20:27-31).

True leadership must point to the lordship of Christ as head of the body of Christ, live as such by example with no hidden agenda, and not shrink back from declaring the whole counsel of God.

Few in leadership have been taken captive by Christ and endured his discipline and training that they may serve only Christ—not please men for their own gain. Most are on ego trips in the pulpit.

Part of effective spiritual warfare is intercessory prayer over God's people whereby the spell of leadership idolatry is broken and the hireling wolf is exposed and chased off. (Thoroughly study Ephesians 4:11-16.)

In these last days God's people are like *"Children, tossed to and fro by the waves and carried about by every wind of doctrine, by human cunning, by craftiness in deceitful schemes"* (Ephesians 4:14). Few believers today know Christ's voice and obey him or walk in maturity becoming equipped to minister the Gospel and in a relationship with Christ where living waters (the Spirit of Christ) flow unhampered through their heart and spirit.

The body of Christ must consist of trained and equipped workers knit together in love where the saving and reviving power of the Holy Spirit works.

Pray earnestly that God would raise up true leadership, fire the hirelings, and that the Lord of the harvest would send out trained workers into these last day white fields, which are ready for the harvest.

A Praying People

When Peter was arrested by Herod, he decided to have Peter executed when realizing that killing Christians pleased the Jews.

Scripture says, *"So Peter was kept in prison, but earnest prayer for him was made to God by the church"* (Acts 12:5).

That sincere, heart wrenching prayer moved the hand of God in such a way that an angel of the Lord was dispatched to rescue Peter from prison and death. Not long after that Herod was killed by an angel of the Lord. The full account is described in Acts12:1-24.

The church of God interceded for Peter's life back then, where are the praying people of God today?

Yes there is a national day of pray, concerts of prayer, a continuous call to intercessory prayer, all manner of books on prayer, prayer meetings, and prayer breakfasts, and the list goes on concerning how we as Christians should all pray.

I believe the main theme for the motive in most prayer throughout the body of Christ is that God maintain America's prosperity—so that God's people have a peaceful, materially blessed, and happy-go-lucky life while on earth.

How lukewarm. So, God is allowing persecution and trouble to remedy the pathetic spiritual state of his people. The days are starting to come upon us where persecution towards Christians will rise to that of the first century Christians as described in the book of Acts.

Soon God's people will have their priorities and motives in prayer aligned with God's will—and once again individual Christians and true fellowships will offer earnest, fervent prayer that moves mountains, opens prison gates, and destroys the wicked—all according to God's perfect will.

A Repeat of Malachi's Prophesy

As stated, so many are confused concerning spiritual warfare, the gifts of the Holy Spirit, sanctification, the rapture, and the Great Tribulation. These and many other confusing issues will soon be cleared up by true servants who will be released to preach the true end-of-the-age sequence of events, along with sound doctrine and expounding on all that Christ taught.

God will raise true leaders and mature workers who will bring the true kingdom of God upon the lost and the deceived, where the true power of God becomes manifest.

Malachi prophesied of the coming day, a day when God acts, and a day when he shines his spotlight upon his true servants.

It is time for those who see the Great Tribulation coming with the need to become prepared, to again fear the Lord—taking no thought for their own comfort. The true servant must step it up and press in and mean business with God and learn to work together, just as Malachi prophesied.

Malachi's prophesy came to pass once with Christ's first coming—and on that day of Pentecost, where the Apostles glorified Christ in the true power of God.

"Then those who feared the LORD spoke with one another; the LORD heeded and heard them, and a book of remembrance was written before him of those who feared the LORD and thought on his name. 'They shall be mine, says the LORD of hosts, <u>my special possession on the day when I act</u>, and I will spare them as a man spares his son who serves him. <u>Then once more you shall distinguish between the righteous and the wicked, between one who serves God and one who does not serve him'</u> (Malachi 3:16-18).

Malachi's prophesy will come to pass again, as this age comes to an end.

5 - Finger of God Power and Prayer

And once again you will see true servants of God demonstrating the true power of Christ and doing battle with hell—effectively exposing darkness and loosening strongholds in people's lives.

You can be part of God's end-of-the-age army and do battle in the power of Christ; if you allow yourself to be cleansed, trained, and disciplined by Christ—not by the doctrines of demons and the teachings of men.

More than ever the true disciple of Christ must know what it means and be willing to do what it takes—to walk in the fullness of Christ doing battle in the power of God's might.

Enlist now!

About the Author

Charles Pretlow has nearly three decades experience in ministry, pastoral counseling and leadership training. He completed his basic Bible classes at Seattle Pacific College and finished his undergraduate work at Central Washington University in Business Administration and Computer Science. His military training in leadership and as an instructor, along with years of coaching athletics adds to a well-rounded approach in leadership instruction, mentoring and training. It was in 1973, while in the Marines, that he came to know Christ and then in 1974 started his ministerial work.

Charles relies on his extensive knowledge and understanding of Scripture, the gifts of the Holy Spirit, and Christ's teachings as well as the work of the Holy Spirit that brings the fullness of Christ to the sincere believer. His approach in shepherding those in his care is companionate, firm, and by example. His preaching, teaching, and discernment is encouraging and uncompromising concerning the false, the game player, and the wolf. He presents Christ's teachings and leadership principles that are often overlooked or avoided. It is the harder words of Christ that when embraced bring death to the carnal self-life, leading to the fullness of life in Christ.

His first published book was in 2004, when he began to write extensively on the sorrowful condition of the body of Christ, the false teachings misleading so many, and the desperate need for true recovery from a crushed spirit and damaged emotions—which can only be worked out in Christ.

Most Christians are not prepared for the coming troubles that God will use to make His church "without spot or blemish" — if you will become rapture ready. Many will be like the five foolish maidens who did not have enough oil for their lamps and missed Christ's appearance. (Matthew 25:1-13). In the end many "on fire" charismatic Christians will find themselves "locked out" from the wedding feast, hearing these words from Christ, "I never knew you; depart from me, you workers of lawlessness" (Mathew 7:23).

This book is dedicated to encourage the sincere believer in Christ to wake up now and get ready, before they hear the midnight cry, "Behold, the bridegroom! Come out to meet him" (Matthew 25:6).

Currently Charles is part of the Message of the Cross International leadership team and one of the pastors ministering at MC Chapel Fellowship in Canon City, Colorado.

Ministry Information

Workshops
www.mccfworkshop.com

MC Chapel Fellowship
The Abbey Campus
(St. Joseph Building - North Section of Campus)
2951 E. Hwy 50
Canon City, CO 81212 - www.mccfcanoncity.com

You are invited to come visit our chapel fellowship and see what God is doing in our lives.

We are a non-denominational fellowship hungry for the true Christ and desiring to grow up in him and become God's people—to love God with all our hearts and worship God in spirit and in truth.

Together we are experiencing God's grace and truth as we seek his will in life and ministry.

If you are seeking sound and meaningful fellowship, without the large crowds, the hype, and entertaining programs—then MC Chapel Fellowship may be God's plan for you.

MORE BOOKS

All the following books are published by Wilderness Voice Publishing, LLC and can be ordered online via Amazon.com or Barnesandnoble.com

The Horsemen Cometh — Gloom, Doom, or Glory
Charles Pretlow   Paperback: 448 pages
ISBN-13: 978-0-980176-80-3

Wake Up Now — Before the Midnight Cry
Charles Pretlow   Paperback: 192 pages
ISBN-13: 978-0-980176-81-0

Discernment
Charles Pretlow   Paperback: 368 pages
ISBN-13: 978-0-980176-84-1

Discernment Companion - Study Guide
Carly   Poe   Paperback: 80 pages
ISBN-13: 978-0-980176-82-7

America on the Brink
Charles Pretlow   Paperback: 34 pages
ISBN-13: 978-0-980176-83-4

Crushed in Spirit
Charles Pretlow   Paperback: 44 pages
ISBN-13: 978-0-980176-89-6

Remember Lot's Wife
Charles Pretlow   Paperback: 34 pages
ISBN-13: 978-0-980176-85-8

God is Raising His Voice
Charles Pretlow   Paperback: 46 pages
Wilderness Voice Publishing, LLC (August 29, 2014)
ISBN-13: 978-0-980176-86-5

In the Power of His Might
Charles Pretlow   Paperback: 102 pages
Wilderness Voice Publishing, LLC (May, 2015)
ISBN-13 978-1-943412-01-3

www.ingramcontent.com/pod-product-compliance
Lightning Source LLC
Chambersburg PA
CBHW030003050426
42451CB00006B/96